£16.99
X

Collins

AQA GCSE

SCIENCE

**FOR AQA GCSE
ADDITIONAL
APPLIED
SCIENCE**

Ken Gadd SERIES EDITOR
Edmund Walsh
Aleksander Jedrosz
Emma Poole
Louise Petheram
David Brodie

William Collins' dream of knowledge for all began with the publication of his first book in 1819. A self-educated mill worker, he not only enriched millions of lives, but also founded a flourishing publishing house. Today, staying true to this spirit, Collins books are packed with inspiration, innovation and a practical expertise. They place you at the centre of a world of possibility and give you exactly what you need to explore it.

Collins. Freedom to teach.

Published by Collins
An imprint of HarperCollinsPublishers
77–85 Fulham Palace Road
Hammersmith
London
W6 8JB

Browse the complete Collins catalogue at
www.collinseducation.com

© HarperCollinsPublishers Limited 2006

10 9 8 7 6 5 4 3 2

ISBN-13 978-0-00-721629-1
ISBN-10 0-00-721629-7

The authors assert their moral right to be identified as the authors of this work.

British Library Cataloguing in Publication Data. A Catalogue record for this publication is available from the British Library.

Commissioned by Cassandra Birmingham

Publishing Manager: Melanie Hoffman

Project Editor: Penny Fowler

Page make-up and picture research by Hart McLeod, Cambridge

Page make-up by eMC Design

Edited by: Sara Hukse, Write Communications

Proof reader: Brian Asbury

Internal design by JPD

Cover design by John Fordham and Starfish

Cover artwork by Bob Lea

Illustrations by Peters and Zabransky, Bob Lea, Stephen Elford, Mike Lacey, Laszlo Veres, Mike Lacey, Peter Cornwell

Production by Natasha Buckland

Printed and bound in Hong Kong by Printing Express Ltd.

Contents

PAGE 15

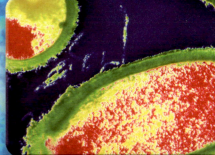

Is this science?

PAGE 49

Are these the key to long life?

PAGE 80

What's this koala got in common with us?

PAGE 98

Modern science can solve ancient mysteries.

PAGE 138

Why does wearing a wet suit keep you warm?

Welcome to Collins GCSE Science!

This book is about scientists – who they are, where they work and what they do. We take you inside the world of food scientists, forensic scientists and sports scientists. You will find out about the skills and knowledge they need to be effective at their jobs.

USING THIS BOOK

What you should know

Think back to what you have already learnt for GCSE Science. You will apply many of these scientific ideas and skills as you find out about scientists at work. We've summarised what you should know for each main section: food science, forensic science and sports science.

Unit opener

Each of the four units begin with an image showing just some of the exciting science you will learn about. Also listed on this page are the spreads you will work through in the unit.

Science in the workplace

In the first unit of this book you will find out what scientists do, where they work and the skills they need. You will also learn about the importance of health and safety in the workplace, including risk assessments, first aid and fire prevention.

There is a unit for each type of scientist, with 12 double page spreads telling you about the particular knowledge and skills they need. This will help you get ready for the written exam, and give you a good understanding of how science works. As you read through a spread, you will start with some basic ideas and be guided to a more detailed understanding of the science. There are questions for you to check your understanding.

Assessed work

As part of your assessment you'll undertake an assignment in one of the three areas. We've given you examples of students' work and shown you what was good and what was less good.

Ideas for investigations

It isn't always easy to think up something to investigate. Your teacher may well suggest the sort of thing you can do. However, to help you we've also given some ideas for investigations.

Unit summary

Key facts and ideas, and the links between them, are summarised in spider diagrams. A really useful way of revising is to make your own concept maps. There is a quiz for you to try and also an activity.

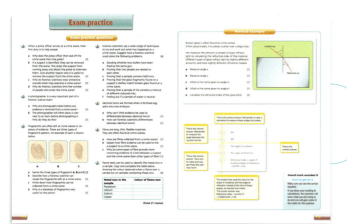

Exam practice

Once you've learned the science, you have to show in an exam what you know and can do. It's important that you understand what the examiner is looking for and that you give your answer as clearly as possible, so we've provided some practice questions.

Why we need food

A balanced diet contains all the nutrients you need to grow and be healthy. It also provides you with the right amount of energy. You need energy to do things like running, playing sport and walking to school. You also need energy to read this page and to sleep. Some activities use more energy than others.

1 What is a balanced diet?
2 Give **three** examples of activities that use up a lot of energy and **three** that use little energy.

Problems caused by too much food

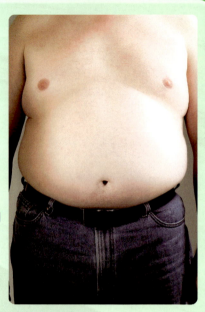

If you eat too much and you take in more energy than you use, you will put on weight. Being very overweight is called being obese. This can lead to various health problems, such as high blood pressure, heart disease, diabetes and arthritis.

3 What does it mean to be obese?
4 Why is it dangerous to be obese?

What is in food

Food consists of carbohydrates, proteins, fats, minerals, vitamins, fibre and water. Food is used as a fuel during respiration to release energy. It also provides the raw materials for growth and repair.

5 Which food groups are used as fuel for respiration?
6 Which food group is important for growth?

Other food problems

Some foods contain substances that cause health problems. Too much salt can lead to an increase in blood pressure. Cholesterol can form blockages in your blood vessels and this increases your chances of getting heart disease. Animal fats (saturated fats) are also a health hazard, though plant fats (unsaturated fats, like sunflower oil) are not so bad.

7 Why is too much salt bad for you?
8 Why are plant fats not so bad for you?

Microorganisms

Microorganisms include bacteria, viruses and some fungi. Those that cause diseases are called pathogens and these include bacteria and viruses. Antibiotics can be used to kill bacteria but not viruses. Scientists have produced lots of different antibiotics to deal with the many different kinds of bacteria.

9 What are microorganisms?

10 Why are antibiotics so useful?

Microbiology

Pathogenic bacteria produce poisonous substances called toxins. It is these toxins that make you feel ill. The problem is that some bacteria have developed a resistance to antibiotics. This means that the antibiotics do not kill them. Even if you complete your course of prescribed antibiotics, you will not get better. Your body will have to rely on its own immune system to get you through.

11 What are pathogens?

12 Explain what toxins are.

Land use

We use land for all sorts of things. We build homes, schools and roads on it. We quarry minerals such as limestone and iron ore out of it. We dump waste in it or all over it and farmers grow crops and keep cattle and sheep on it.

13 Suggest something else that we build on the land.

14 Why do farmers grow crops and keep cattle on the land?

Growing plants

Intensive farming uses lots of fertilisers and pesticides. These increase the production of crops. Plants need various things for growth, including light, water and carbon dioxide from the air.

15 Why do intensive farmers use herbicides?

16 Name **two** things that plants need to grow.

Atoms

Elements are made of just one type of atom. There are only about a hundred different elements. Compounds consist of two or more different types of atom that have been joined together. Atoms can be joined together by sharing electrons or by giving and taking electrons.

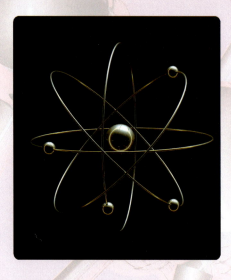

1 What is special about an element?
2 How can atoms join together to form compounds?

Cells

Plants and animals are made up of cells. Animal cells have a nucleus, a cell membrane and cytoplasm. Humans have many specialised cells, including red blood cells and sperm cells.

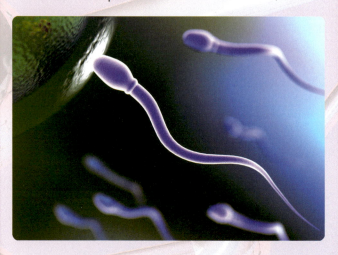

3 Name **three** parts of an animal cell.
4 Name **two** specialised animal cells.

Microscopes

A microscope can be used to look at very small objects such as cells or samples of fabrics or hair. A microscope allows us to see a magnified image of the object.

5 What are microscopes used to see?
6 Why does a microscope allow you to see details better?

Inherited features

People have different features. Some of our features, such as eye colour, are caused by genetic information that has been inherited from our parents. We say that these are inherited features. Other features, such as scars, are caused by the way we lead our lives. We say that these are environmental features.

7 Name **one** inherited feature.
8 Name **one** environmental feature.

Blood

Blood is part of the body's circulatory system. It transports oxygen and nutrients around the body. Blood is pumped

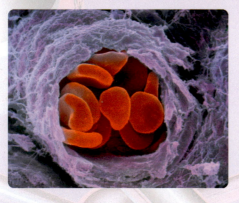

around the body by the heart. There are three types of blood vessels:

- Arteries, which carry blood away from the heart
- Veins, which carry blood back to the heart
- Capillaries, which are tiny blood vessels that connect the arteries and veins together

9   What does blood do?
10 Which blood vessels carry blood away from the heart?

Solutions

Some substances dissolve in liquids to form solutions. For example, salt dissolves in water to form salt water. The substance that dissolves is known as the solute and the liquid in which it dissolves is the solvent.

11 A blue ink dissolves in water. Is the ink or the water the solvent?
12 What is a mixture of a solvent and a solute called?

Refraction

Light passes through transparent materials like glass. This makes glass a very useful material for making objects such as windows and doors. Light is bent, or refracted, as it passes from one transparent material to another. So light is refracted as it travels from air to glass.

13 Name **two** transparent materials.
14 What happens when light passes from air to glass?

Dispersion

We call the light that comes from the Sun white light. In fact, white light is a mixture of red, orange, yellow, green, blue, indigo and violet light. White light can be split into a spectrum using a glass block called a prism. We call this process dispersion.

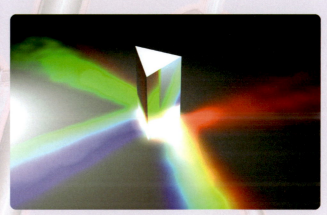

15 What is white light made up from?
16 What is the name of the glass block used to split white light?

Food as fuel

You know that all living things need energy, and that we get our energy from the food we eat. The energy we get from our food is used to keep us warm, to keep our body processes running and to keep us active. The more active we are, the more energy we will use. If we take in more energy than we use, we will put on weight because the extra energy is stored as fat. If we use more energy than we take in, we will suffer malnutrition and eventually starve.

1 List at least **three** things that we use energy for.
2 What factors affect how much energy we need to take in?

Food types

Different types of food supply us with different benefits. We say they contain different nutrients.

Starchy foods such as bread, potatoes, rice and pasta contain carbohydrates, which are good for giving us energy. Fatty or oily foods give us energy too, and they are needed to make nerve and brain cells and cell membranes. Meat, eggs, nuts and pulses contain protein that is needed to build new cells, and for hormones and enzymes. Fruit and vegetables contain vitamins and minerals that are needed to keep all the body processes working well.

3 Name **two** or more food types that are good for supplying energy.
4 Why do we need to eat fruit and vegetables?

A balanced diet

A balanced diet supplies the right amounts of all the different types of nutrients we need. Many people in the UK do not eat enough vitamins and minerals, and many eat too many calories or too much salt or fat. Eating the wrong amount of food, or the wrong types of food, contributes to health problems such as heart disease or cancer. Experts say most of our calories should come from carbohydrates, and about 25% of our calories from fat. We should eat at least five portions of fruit or vegetables each day.

5 Describe some of the ways in which many people in the UK eat an unhealthy diet.
6 Discuss the benefits of eating plenty of fruit and vegetables.

Heart and circulation

You can feel your pulse rate at your wrist or your neck. It tells you how fast your heart is beating. Your heart pumps blood rich in oxygen from your lungs, through blood vessels called arteries and capillaries, to all the cells in your body. After the blood has passed through cells, it is pumped through blood vessels called veins back to your lungs. When you exercise, your cells need more oxygen, so your heart pumps faster and your pulse rate increases.

7 When is your blood rich in oxygen? When does it have less oxygen?
8 Work together to draw a sketch diagram to show how your blood flows around your body.

Breathing and respiration

Sometimes people confuse 'breathing' and 'respiration'. Breathing is when muscles move our ribs in and out, and our diaphragm up and down, so that air is drawn 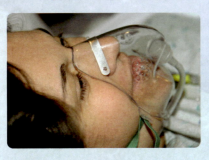 into our lungs and then breathed out again. In our lungs, oxygen from the air passes into our blood and waste carbon dioxide from our blood passes into our lungs, and we breathe it out. Respiration is a chemical reaction that happens in all the cells in our body. Glucose and oxygen are used in the cells to produce energy. The waste products are water and carbon dioxide.

9 Describe what happens in our lungs.
10 Write a word equation to show what happens during respiration.

Muscles

Without muscles we could not move! But we could not do a lot of other things as well. Muscles are used in our heart to pump blood round our body, in our chest to make us breathe, and to move food through our digestive system. Muscles are made of special cells that contract or get shorter, and then relax again. So muscles can pull, but they can't push. To move joints like our knee or our elbow, we need two sets of muscles: one set to make the joint bend (or flex), and a different set to straighten it out again.

11 List the uses of muscles in our bodies.
12 Describe briefly how a joint such as the knee or the elbow works.

Friction

Friction is very important in the design of lots of pieces of equipment. When there is a lot of friction between two different surfaces, they do not slide over each other, but if there is little friction, they will slide over each other easily. The rougher surfaces are, the more friction there will be between them. Sometimes friction is useful, such as between the sole of a trainer and a running track, or on bicycle brakes. Sometimes we need to reduce friction, such as between an ice skate blade and the ice, or in the bearings of a bicycle wheel.

13 Give **one** example of your own where friction is useful, and **one** where it is a nuisance.
14 Suggest **one** or more ways to reduce the friction between two surfaces.

Polymers

There is a vast number of different materials, but only a relatively small number of elements. Chemists are able to make new materials by combining the chemical elements in new ways to make new compounds. Most of the new materials are polymers – they are made from long chains of atoms bound together. The different ways atoms and molecules bind together give the different materials different properties, so chemists can design polymers to be strong, or flexible, or stretchy, or hard, depending on what they want to use the material for.

15 Why are there many materials but only relatively few chemical elements?
16 Explain in your own words what a 'polymer' is.

WORK LIKE A SCIENTIST!

Over 40% of higher education students study science or engineering.

Nearly 40% of qualified scientists and engineers are female.

Science is involved in a multitude of industries, including pharmaceuticals, chemicals, biotechnology and petrochemicals, with job roles from testing and developing medicines, plastics or detergents, to environmental or cancer research.

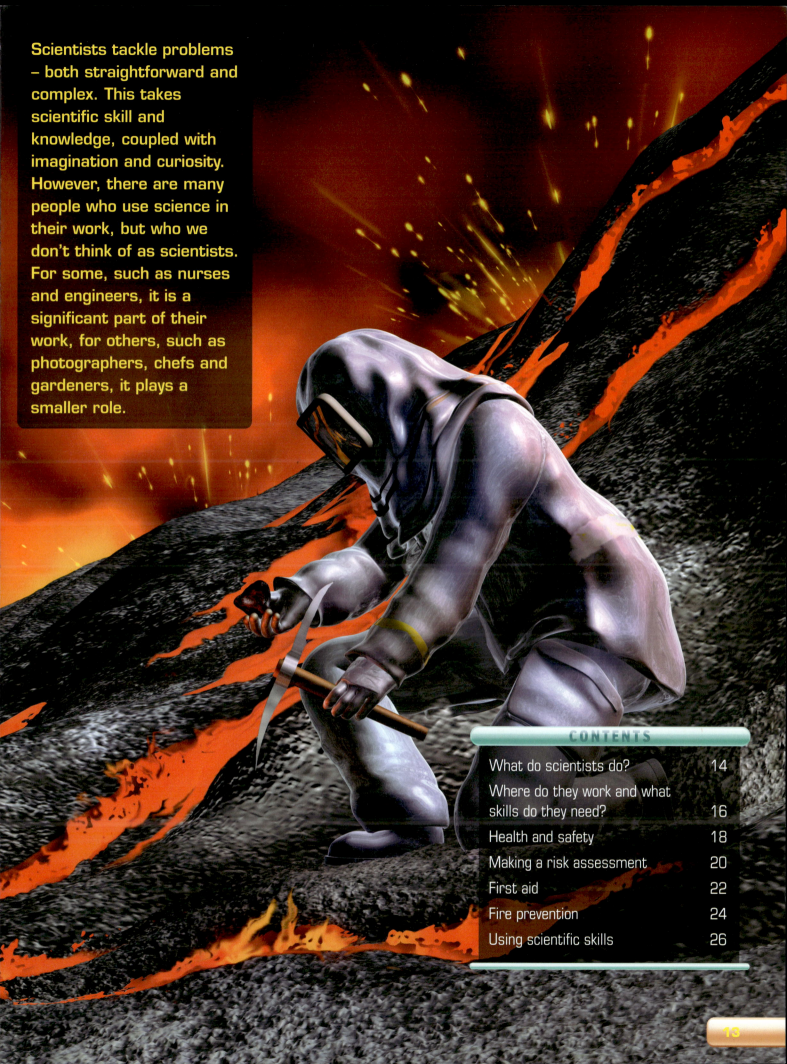

Scientists tackle problems – both straightforward and complex. This takes scientific skill and knowledge, coupled with imagination and curiosity. However, there are many people who use science in their work, but who we don't think of as scientists. For some, such as nurses and engineers, it is a significant part of their work, for others, such as photographers, chefs and gardeners, it plays a smaller role.

CONTENTS

What do scientists do?

Scientists can do a tremendously wide range of jobs. Most of them do not wear white coats and many of them do not work in laboratories. Very few of them make explosives. So what do they do?

Scientists are people that use scientific ideas to make certain things possible. Scientists make it possible for electricity to be supplied cheaply and reliably and for food to be safe and nutritious. They make medical procedures possible and enable drugs to be supplied that will make you better if you are ill. They make sense of the evidence that tells us more about how the world came about – and how it may end.

"I'm Brian and I'm a Development Manager for a china clay company. China clay is used to make toothpaste and ceramics and to put a gloss on paper. My job is to develop new uses for china clay. I lead a team and travel the world to share ideas with other parts of the company. I have a science degree, though I also need other skills, like leadership and communication. Sometimes the team gets a bit down if a project doesn't work out, and it's my job to motivate them. My reports have to be easily understood and accurate."

"I'm Sumathi and I'm a college science technician. I prepare solutions and equipment for demonstrations and practicals. You have to be precise in this job; a solution has to be the correct strength and some chemicals are unpleasant so you have to know the correct way to handle them. There's a lot of satisfaction though in getting it right. I have a BTEC qualification, but you can pick up the people skills you need as you go along. Some staff are very knowledgeable about what's needed for a demonstration, others need more support from me. That takes tact but I know they appreciate the support."

"I'm Sue and I'm a radiographer at the local hospital. I operate equipment such as X-ray machines and ultrasound scanners. I'm trained to BTEC level, but there's sometimes a new piece of equipment and we have to be trained in it there and then. I love working with the patients – they're sometimes quite nervous so it's important I put them at their ease. Some images take skill to interpret and it's great being able to show people what's what. I have to understand the health and safety angle. Overdoses are serious – for staff as well!"

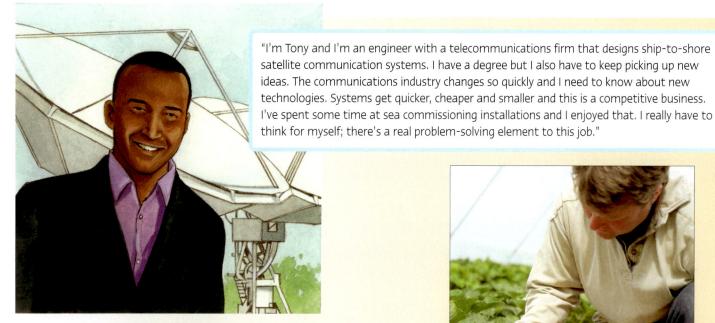

"I'm Tony and I'm an engineer with a telecommunications firm that designs ship-to-shore satellite communication systems. I have a degree but I also have to keep picking up new ideas. The communications industry changes so quickly and I need to know about new technologies. Systems get quicker, cheaper and smaller and this is a competitive business. I've spent some time at sea commissioning installations and I enjoyed that. I really have to think for myself; there's a real problem-solving element to this job."

"I'm Alison, I'm a hair stylist and I love my job. I just love making people look good. If you look good you feel positive and that motivates you to do things. I did an NVQ at college and I got diplomas in other skills, such as colouring. I was surprised to use science in my course but you have to know about chemicals and the skin. Some of the products I use give off vapours that can affect you – hydrogen peroxide is one I don't like."

"I'm Raymond and I run a 'Pick Your Own' fruit business. I used to be a farmer and learned how to grow crops from my parents. The farm didn't make much money though, so I just keep a few fields to grow fruit. The fruit grows itself and the customers pick it themselves! Mind you, I could lose the whole lot to pests – or all my customers to the supermarkets. The soil has to be right, and so does the spraying. I have to match the plants to the climate here and the soil."

ACTIVITIES

1 Working in small groups, get a large sheet of paper and divide it into columns.
   a You will need a column for each of the scientists featured on this spread. Put their name at the top of their column and add their job title.
   b In each column put the word 'local', 'national' or 'international' to describe the kind of organisation they work for.
   c Now write a sentence for each person, explaining how they use science to do their job.
   d Indicate what level of qualification or training they have.
   e Write a sentence for each explaining how they make a contribution to society.
   f Finally, add the word 'major', 'significant' or 'small' to indicate the role that science plays in the work of that organisation.

2 Decide which of these organisations could be active in the area you live in.

3 Choose **one** of the people in this activity. If they moved into your area and couldn't get a job doing exactly the same as they had before, what do you think they could use their skills to do instead?

4 Set up a spider chart with the words 'scientific skills' in the centre. Add to it the various scientific skills that these scientists possess. You might start with ones like 'understand the uses of chemicals'.

5 Now set up another spider chart with the words 'other skills' in the centre and add skills that these people have that are not specific to science. You could start with 'good at communication'.

Where do they work and what skills do they need?

Organisations that use science may be local, national or international.

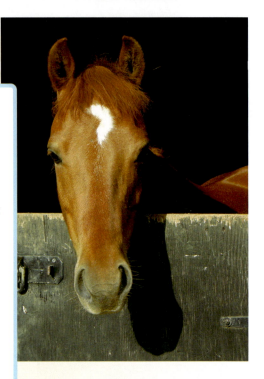

Mitchell Hill Veterinary Centre

Mitchell Hill Veterinary Centre is a local business that specialises in large animal care and treatment. They have four vets who travel around to farms and stables.

Jonathan, the senior partner, has been a vet for 19 years and has seen a lot of changes in that time. "Some of the new drugs are tremendous but it all comes down to some pretty key ideas. We think of animals in terms of systems, such as digestive or reproductive, and we have to understand the functions of the organs, such as the stomach or the womb."

Vets can diagnose and treat illnesses, but sometimes samples have to be sent away for testing. "The guys at the labs have to be good with a microscope – recognising the difference between a healthy cell and a diseased one is crucial."

"When a farmer or stable owner calls us out they want to be sure we can do our job; they need that animal to get better so it can earn its keep. We play an essential role in keeping those businesses open."

Carvoza Cuisine

Carvoza Cuisine is a national business providing restaurants with processed food which is ready to cook and serve. They have food processing factories, storage depots and a fleet of refrigerated delivery trucks. Lisa, their Food Hygiene Manager, says, "Our food has to be healthy and tasty."

They buy ingredients such as pasta and vegetables and cook meals such as lasagne. These are frozen and stored ready for distribution. "Microbes can cause diseases and they grow well in warm food. Food has to be cooked thoroughly, which kills the microbes, and then frozen, which stops more microbes from growing."

"Although much of the food processing is automated, the quality control is done by hand. We have a lot of drivers and sales people. We have to keep visiting many of the restaurants we sell to, to encourage them to keep ordering from us." The processing factories are in industrial estates on the edge of large towns, often close to motorway junctions.

Zircon International

Zircon International is a telecommunications firm using a range of technologies, including mobile phone networks and satellite links. "This is a truly scientific business", says Managing Director, Jaan. "We have teams of scientists applying their understanding of waves to increase our network."

The shape of the land makes a big difference to the work they do. "We have to position our masts to give really good coverage, but without putting up too many, which would push up costs and cause complaints. That means knowing about reflection and refraction. We have satellite links to North America and to the Indian Ocean area, so we have people out there to maintain the system. These are important areas for businesses, so we can make money out of them, but the communications links help other organisations as well."

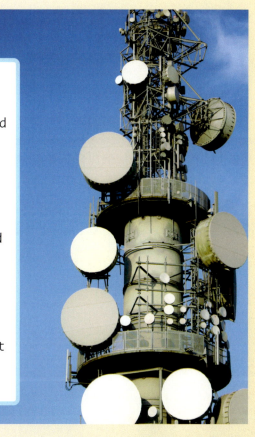

1   Which of these businesses is:
    a   international?
    b   national?
    c   local?

2   Think about businesses in your area that use science. Can you find one to fit each of the categories in **1**?

3   Design a table to show some information about the three organisations you have named in **2**. It might look like this:

4   Find out what careers are available in science and science-related areas in the region you live in. The following websites should help you:
    www.newscientistjobs.com
    www.doctorjob.com/science

	Organisation A	Organisation B	Organisation C
Local, national or international?			
Type of scientific activity carried out?			
Why is that activity important to society?			
Where are they based?			
Why are they based there?			
Are they a major, significant or small user of science?			

Health and safety

It is the responsibility of everyone to behave in a way that is healthy and safe. Science laboratories have a very good safety record and very few people are injured or killed in them. However, that is only because most people are careful and sensible. Accidents can and do happen.

In this picture there are a number of situations that are potentially hazardous.

1 Look at the picture carefully and identify the hazards. You should be able to find eight. Discuss and decide what is unsafe, what might go wrong and what should be done to remedy it. Then put your findings into a table. Your table might look something like this:

Hazard no.	Hazard	Danger	Remedy
1	Reagent bottle near edge of bench	Bottle might be knocked off, smashed and chemical spilt	Move bottle to safer place, such as centre of bench if in use or returned to store if not.
2			
3			
4			

2 Match the signs to their meanings and give an example of each from the list on the right:

- Irritant
- Toxic
- Oxidising
- Highly flammable
- Corrosive
- Microorganisms
- Risk of electric shock

- Concentrated sulfuric acid
- Potassium nitrate
- Salmonella
- Mains supply
- Ethanol
- Calcium hydroxide
- Lead nitrate

Radioactive materials

Radioactive materials have various uses. These include smoke detectors, medical diagnosis and preserving fruit. These and other applications involve the handling of radioactive materials. It is important that people do this safely, are not exposed to too great a risk and that radioactive waste is disposed of properly.

1 In many schools, teachers have access to radioactive sources. On post-16 courses, students may use the sources to carry out experiments. The radioactive sources are subject to regulations and legal controls. Ask your teacher for a briefing sheet on the use of radioactive sources. Examine it carefully. Your task is to design a reminder sheet to go in the exercise book of a student who uses radioactive sources.

2 Some workers use radioactive materials on a regular basis. It is important to monitor their exposure. You might use books or the Internet, but in either case some useful starting points might be to look up references to radiation dosimeters (devices people use to monitor their exposure to radiation). Write a paragraph or two, with an illustration, to explain how people who are regularly exposed to ionising radiation make sure they are not over-exposed.

3 Many different things count as radioactive waste. They are generally grouped into three categories – low, medium and high. See what you can find out about each in order to complete this table. Some of it has been completed already.

	Low-level waste	Medium-level waste	High-level waste
Examples	Used protective clothing and tools from areas where radioactivity is used.		
Does it need to be shielded to protect people?	No		
Produced by			Nuclear reactors
Disposed of by		Solidified in concrete or bitumen	

Making a risk assessment

Health and safety is an important aspect of life today. This includes when we are working as scientists. It doesn't necessarily mean:

- filling in lots of forms (although sometimes it is a good idea to write things down)
- that we are going to be stopped from doing things we want to (although we may have to change our plans).

What it does mean is managing the risk and reducing it to an acceptable level.

Health and Safety at Work

In Britain, the Health & Safety Executive is responsible for ensuring safe practices are planned and observed. They have the power to enforce good practice. Their job is to reduce the likelihood of you or the people you work with being injured or killed at work.

The Management of Health & Safety at Work Regulations make it clear that:

- by law you have to work in a way that is safe
- you have to work towards the safety of others
- managers have to play their part as well.

The Control of Substances Hazardous to Health (COSHH) Regulations limit your exposure to dangerous substances.

Risk assessments

A risk assessment is a reasoned examination of an activity that could cause people harm. It consists of:

- an assessment of the probability of an accident happening
- an assessment of the consequences of that accident happening.

The risk assessment is a judgement based on the probability and the consequences.

The probability and consequences are often quite different in terms of size. For example, the probability of being struck by lightning is very low, but the consequences are very great. The probability of getting water in your eyes when you go swimming is very high, but the consequences are probably very small. Neither of these would therefore be considered particularly risky. However, crossing a road with your eyes closed would rank high, both in terms of probability and consequences, which is why we wouldn't do it.

Teachers organising school trips have to carry out risk assessments (or use prepared ones), and if the risk is too great the activity has to be modified or avoided.

In order to reduce the risk from a particular hazard to an acceptable level, it may be necessary to adopt one or more control measures (precautions). In school science, this might involve wearing appropriate eye protection, doing an activity in the fume cupboard, using a more dilute solution or a lower voltage, quickly wiping up a spill, using sterile technique in microbiology, etc. Other control measures might require thorough training before an activity takes place, warning labels or signs in appropriate places or locking up hazardous materials.

A risk assessment that a teacher might do for a school experiment is shown on the next page.

Tregannel High School
RISK ASSESSMENT For Growing Copper Sulfate Crystals

Name of Assessor: Julie Ellis   Assessor's Signature: ......J. Ellis...........   Date October 26th 2006

Activity/ Process/ Operation	What are the Hazards to Health and Safety?	What are your sources of information about these hazards?	What could go wrong? Who could be affected?	What control measures (precautions) can be taken to reduce the risk?	Risk Level Achieved High/ Medium/Low	What further action is needed to reduce the risk?
Evaporating water from saturated solution of copper sulfate to grow crystals	Saturated solutions of copper sulfate are harmful and are an irritant	CLEAPSS Student Safety Sheets, personal experience, bottle label	There is a risk of the solution being swallowed by a student, causing poisoning, and of some of the solution being splashed on skin, causing irritation.	The containers have been labelled "harmful" and students have been briefed on the meaning of hazard symbols previously. It will be explained to the students at the start of the lesson what the risks are, what they should and shouldn't do, and what to do if there is an accident.	Low	None. This is a responsible and sensible group who will listen to instructions and follow them.

ACTIVITIES

Consider each of these activities. Discuss the probability of something going wrong, the consequences of it going wrong and what should then happen. Then copy and complete the table below. The first row has been completed for you.

1   The rubber tubing on a Bunsen burner has started to become brittle and crack at the ends.

2   A power pack has a chafed mains lead connecting it to the power supply.

3   Dilute hydrochloric acid has been spilt on a bench top and not cleaned up.

4   A piece of bread has gone mouldy and is sealed in a Petri dish.

Activity	Probability of something going wrong	Consequences of it going wrong	What should happen
1	Considerable – if unburned gas starts leaking out	Severe – gas could ignite from the Bunsen flame and would have a continuous fuel supply	Burner should be immediately removed from service and the tubing replaced
2			
3			
4			

The purpose of a risk assessment is, of course, to make sure that people behave in a safe way and that, as far as possible, accidents do not happen.

In each of these situations, something has gone wrong. Your task is to suggest how the working practice of the workplace should be changed.

1   A group of students is thermally decomposing (breaking down with heat) carbonates, most of which are white powders. Charlene's group has done calcium carbonate and magnesium carbonate. They know that they are supposed to do some more and find another white powder in an unlabelled jar. Upon heating, this white powder ignites and burns vigorously, shattering the boiling tube.

2   A class has been doing an experiment that involves heating solutions in boiling tubes. The students wore goggles and the boiling tubes were clamped at an angle. Sam's group has finished their practical work, cleared their equipment away (including the goggles) and are writing up their notes from the experiment. The group working on the row behind is still doing their experiment. Suddenly the liquid in the boiling tube boils up, flies out of the tube and sprays over Sam.

3   Salim's group is doing a lesson that involves watching a video and making notes. As they came in the room the previous class was clearing up after some practical work; students were putting chemicals away and wiping the benches down with wet cloths. The benches felt a bit damp at the start, but they soon dried. However, partway through the lesson, Salim felt the edges of his hands (where they had been in contact with the bench) start to itch. He rubbed his hands on his clothes, but that made the irritation worse.

First aid

The number of injuries and deaths in science laboratories, and workplaces where science is used, is very small. But the risk is still present.

First aid can:
- **save lives**
- **provide comfort to victims.**
- **reduce the severity of injuries**

It doesn't necessitate large amounts of time in training; a few basic skills and an understanding based on advice from professionals provide a good basis.

There are also a number of misconceptions about what should be done in certain cases and a well-intentioned but misinformed first aider can do more harm than good.

Common injuries that can happen in laboratories include the following.

Heat burns and scalds

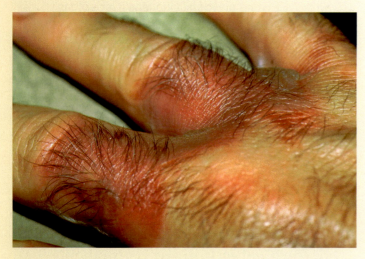

Burns are caused by dry heat, such as a Bunsen burner flame; scalds are caused by wet heat, such as boiling water.

The casualty will experience pain and possibly shock. Symptoms include swelling, blisters and redness. The priorities are to try to reduce the pain and the risk of infection. Cold water should be applied for several minutes and a dressing applied. If the burn is at all serious, call 999. Nothing should be applied to the injury other than water or a dressing.

Chemical burns

Some chemicals may burn the skin if they come in contact with it. These may be liquids, such as a concentrated acid, or powders, such as lime.

The priorities are to remove the cause of the injury and to prevent infection. The cause of the burn should be removed, either with cool running water for at least 15 minutes in the case of a liquid, or brushing in the case of a powder. Any contaminated clothing or jewellery should be removed and the affected area wrapped loosely with a clean dressing or cloth. Minor burns usually heal themselves; however if there are symptoms of shock, such as fainting or shallow breathing, or if the burn is deeper, or has affected the eyes or face, hands or feet, groin or buttocks, seek expert attention.

Injury from breathing in fumes or swallowing chemicals

Many chemicals in use in scientific activities are potentially dangerous if swallowed. Any such chemical should have the appropriate hazard symbol on it and should be treated with respect. Some chemicals, such as ammonia, release fumes that are dangerous.

Symptoms vary according to what has been swallowed, but may include drowsiness or unconsciousness, nausea and vomiting, and even cardiac arrest.

It is important (as always in first aid) to see if the danger is still present, such as the source of fumes. The priorities are to ensure that the casualty's airway is open and to call an ambulance. If the casualty isn't responding, resuscitation may be necessary.

Do not attempt to induce vomiting as this may block the airway. If the chemical that has caused the injury is known, this should be communicated when making the 999 call and to the ambulance crew.

Electric shock

Low voltages (typically around 12 V) present few risks, but mains voltage can be lethal. If an electric current passes through the body, it can cause breathing and heartbeat to stop.

Recovery cannot begin if the casualty is still in contact with the source of the current, and the first aider is at risk of shock as well.

Removing the source of current, if necessary, may be done by switching off the supply or using an insulator such as a wooden broom. If unconscious, a casualty's airway should be opened and resuscitation may be appropriate. An ambulance should be called.

Cuts and damage to the eyes from particles or chemicals

In the case of a chemical splash in the eye, the priority is to thoroughly remove the harmful liquid. The affected eye or eyes should be flushed with clean lukewarm water for at least 20 minutes. Remember that the same chemical may be on other parts of the body, such as the hands. The eyes are the priority but it is necessary to avoid re-contamination by washing hands.

It is important not to allow the casualty to rub his or her eyes as this will increase the damage or allow any other liquids to be introduced.

If foreign particles enter the eye, the priority is to remove them. There are three established ways of doing this:

- Let tears wash out the particle.
- Use an eye wash.
- Pull the upper lid down onto the lower lid and let the lower eyelashes sweep away the particles by blinking repeatedly.

If this doesn't work, the eye should be closed and immediate expert attention sought. It is essential that the eye is not rubbed.

ACTIVITIES

1 Discuss and decide on a series of bullet points for action in each of the following cases.
  a Jamal is working with his group to clear away the equipment from a practical lesson. They have been using Bunsen burners and tripods; he picks up a tripod and immediately drops it. The burner had only just been turned off and moved away; the tripod was extremely hot.
  b Rod was reaching down behind a steel filing cabinet to retrieve something that had fallen down there and accidentally touched a cable. The cable had been damaged by the cabinet and the insulation no longer surrounded the wires. Rod is unconscious and slumped against the cabinet.

  c Sarah is complaining of sore eyes. She has been handling a number of chemicals, some of which are labelled as 'irritant', and has been wearing goggles. However, the goggles are uncomfortable and she has been rubbing her eyes. She complains that the more she rubs them, the worse they feel.

2 Explain why it is important in a place of work where scientific equipment and materials are in use for someone to be a trained first aider.

3 Find out which organisations can provide training in first aid skills and how to contact them.

Fire prevention

Generally speaking, fire causes far more injuries and deaths in the home than at work. Only 6% of deaths and 10% of injuries occur in the workplace. However, we mustn't be complacent. These figures are so low because the right equipment is provided and people behave sensibly.

If you hear a fire alarm or smoke alarm:

- Make sure all windows are closed, doors shut (do not lock them as they may impede the emergency services) and all gas or electrical supplies turned off.
- Leave the building immediately via the nearest exit; do not stop to collect personal belongings.
- Do not use lifts in case the power supply fails.
- Wheelchair users should wait in the designated areas at the head of stairs; a responsible person should be informed.

If you find a fire:

- Break the glass of the nearest fire alarm.
- Dial 999 direct. Give your name and details of where you are, and the position and size of the fire.
- Provided that there is no personal risk and you feel confident to do so, attack the fire using appropriate fire extinguishers.

How fire doors function

Fire doors delay the spread of fire and smoke without hindering movement. Their function is to reduce the passage of smoke during the early stages of a fire and to provide a barrier to a well-developed fire without permitting flames and lots of smoke to pass.

Some doors are only required to fulfil the first function as they may not be subjected to the full severity of a fire; these are smoke stop doors. Others may have the main aim of resisting fire penetration; these are fire-resisting doors. Some may have to meet both requirements.

It should be understood how important it is that such doors are not wedged open. An open fire door cannot prevent smoke from travelling quickly around a building, nor can it contain a fire long enough to give occupants time to escape.

Automatic sprinkler systems

Each sprinkler head is held closed by heat-sensitive seals, which prevent water flow until a set temperature is exceeded. 'Wet' systems have water already pressurised in the pipes. These systems require no manual controls to activate, as long as adequate water supplies are provided.

'Pre-action' systems are designed for locations such as museums or libraries where accidental use must be avoided. Valves are connected to devices such as smoke detectors or heat detectors and virtually eliminate the possibility of accidental triggering.

'Deluge' systems are 'pre-action' systems in which every sprinkler will discharge water. This ensures a large and simultaneous application of water over the entire hazard. These systems are used for special hazards where rapid fire spread is a concern.

Different types of fire extinguisher (water, carbon dioxide, dry powder, foam) are used on different types of fire.

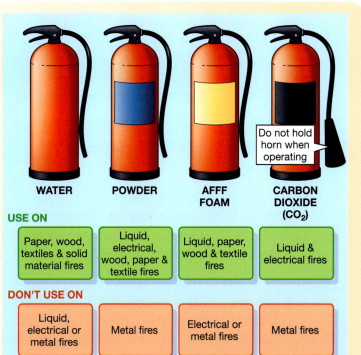

Do not hold horn when operating

WATER	POWDER	AFFF FOAM	CARBON DIOXIDE (CO_2)
USE ON			
Paper, wood, textiles & solid material fires	Liquid, electrical, wood, paper & textile fires	Liquid, paper, wood & textile fires	Liquid & electrical fires
DON'T USE ON			
Liquid, electrical or metal fires	Metal fires	Electrical or metal fires	Metal fires

Another way of extinguishing a fire is to use a fire blanket. This is a sheet of fire-resistant material that can be used to cover a fire to cut off its supply of oxygen. They are quick to use and easy to maintain but can only be used on a small, contained fire. You have to move in close to the fire and your hands are vulnerable; it may be difficult to retrieve the blanket for another go at putting out the fire.

FIRE BLANKET

PULL TAPES

ACTIVITIES

1   Design a credit card-sized reminder card, or a bookmark, which includes essential information about fire prevention. Keep it brief, but don't miss out essential details.

2   You are on a work placement in a large office building that consists of several connected blocks. In the corridors between the blocks are swing doors that have to be pushed open to pass through. Some staff find them a nuisance, especially if they are carrying bulky items.
   a   What is the function of these doors?
   b   One day someone decides to fold a piece of paper into a wedge shape and push it under one of the doors. Why is this not a good idea?
   c   In some buildings, doors like this are held open with electromagnets. Research on the Internet to find out what would happen to these in the event of a fire.

3   Which kind of sprinkler system would you recommend for:
   a   an art gallery
   b   a warehouse used to store cardboard for packing glass bulbs
   c   a hotel?

4   Which kind of extinguisher or blanket would you use on:
   a   someone who has spilt methanol on their sleeve and it has caught alight
   b   burning rubbish in a waste paper basket
   c   a burning electrical appliance such as a TV?

Using scientific skills

You need to produce a portfolio of evidence about:

- **workplaces that use science**
- **how science and scientific skills are used in the workplace.**

You need to consider safety precautions in the workplace and compare these with the health and safety precautions in your school or college. You should use a variety of sources of information and present your findings in a clear and logical way.

Your portfolio of evidence should include the following:

- **A report of an investigation into workplaces that use scientific skills, describing the work of scientists or those who use scientific skills, and how science is important in a wide variety of jobs.**
- **A report of an investigation into working safely in a scientific workplace and a comparison with the health and safety precautions in your school or college.**

Below is an example of a report on a workplace. It isn't perfect and wouldn't get full marks, but the student writing it did try to cover all the aspects that were expected.

My workplace report on Tregannel Zoo

For my workplace report I visited Tregannel Zoo. I had worked there for two weeks for my work experience so I knew quite a lot about how it is run. I had a lot of help from the staff there.

The zoo is in the centre of Tregannel, which is a popular seaside resort. Being in the centre means that it is very easy for holidaymakers who are staying in the town to get to it. A lot of other visitors to the area go into the town, especially if it isn't good weather for the beach, so the zoo gets a lot of visitors so that it gets the money it needs to stay open. Because it is not near the seafront it doesn't get the strong winds and also the noise from people on the seafront in the evening, so the animals are not frightened.

Jo has described and explained its location here very well. Perhaps a map might help as well.

It has a wide range of animals, though not many very big ones as there isn't a great deal of space and it wouldn't be fair on them. The animals all have to be housed in suitable accommodation. They have to have bedding and food and medical attention. Visitors who come to the zoo want to know about the animals so there has to be signs and guides. The zoo also has special events, such as evening opening in the winter so that visitors can see the nocturnal animals come out. The zoo is very important as it is a major tourist attraction in a town that depends on visitors. People coming to visit the zoo often go to other things as well so lots of people benefit. Also the zoo has to buy things it needs so that local businesses can sell it things like food for visitors and food for the animals.

Jo has described the services provided and explained their importance to society very well – she clearly talked to the staff and thought about the town. She could develop this further by thinking about whether the zoo has a negative impact, such as competing with smaller businesses such as cafés.

The zoo has its own vet as some of the animals are very unusual. He is called Richard and he trained in Bristol. He worked at London Zoo and at a safari park before he came to Tregannel. They have a lot of keepers and they all specialise in a different part of the zoo, for example Katy looks after the penguins and the other large birds. She knows all the penguins by name and knows if they are not feeling well just by looking at them. All the keepers have to know about other parts of the zoo as well for when other keepers have days off.

Jo has given an account of the skills and qualifications needed by scientists who work there and has realised that there are different levels of expertise needed. She can develop this further by being more specific about the qualifications and other skills needed.

The effect the zoo has on the local environment is both positive and negative. On the one hand it is nicely cared for and well planted with lots of different plants to make it look natural and pleasant. The visitors like this and so do the animals as many of them like shelter. On the other hand the zoo is very popular so lots of visitors come and most of them come by car so there are the exhaust fumes and the big car park, but I suppose that many of them would come to Tregannel anyway.

Health and safety is very important at the zoo and I had to be given a lot of training even for work experience. One of the main risks is with some of the animals, who might attack if frightened, and some of them carry diseases. Katy told me about the parrots. They have a pair of African Greys who are older than she is and are called Jeremy and Alex (Alex is short for Alexandra). They are beautiful but there is a risk of psittacosis if you get a bad peck from them.

Jo has described the effect on the local environment of the organisation with thought and has realised that there are both positive and negative effects. She could develop these with more detail and maybe use some illustrations.

All the keepers have to know what risks there are from each animal as well as from really simple things like slipping on wet paving stones or cutting yourself with a knife when you're getting feeds ready. They have first aid kits all over the place and they're checked regularly. All the keepers are qualified first aiders in case visitors need attention. I didn't think that fire would be a big risk there but it is because there have to be plans about what to do with the animals. The first priority is to get visitors out and then to deal with the animals. They are all trained in this. Health and safety there is like it is at school in some ways but not in others. On the one hand we have first aid kits and first aiders and you have to know what the dangers are. On the other hand it's different because even in Science and DT we don't have anything as dangerous as lions! Also we have to keep learning about new hazards every time we do a new experiment, but they've always got the same ones.

Jo has carried out research into the issues of working safely in a scientific workplace and compared these with her school laboratory, including hazards and risks and their assessment, first aid and fire prevention. She has included a lot of detail and has obviously learned a lot by asking questions and listening carefully. She could develop this further by finding out, for example, whether the regulations and guidelines for small animals in a zoo are the same as they are if kept in school.

I really enjoyed being at the zoo – it was fun and everyone was really helpful.

Jo Ellis

Jo has identified and used a range of sources and information to present her findings clearly throughout her portfolio. Much of her information came straight from the staff that she worked with and this can now be supplemented from a wider range of views.

Food science

DISCOVER FOOD, GLORIOUS FOOD!

What you eat has a direct effect on your health. If you are not eating enough of the right foods or are eating too much of the wrong ones, your health will suffer. Heart disease is one of the biggest causes of death in the UK and can be caused directly by poor diet. Eating a balanced diet can prevent many other problems too, including weak bones, bad skin and low energy levels.

Carbohydrates provide you with energy, but if you eat more than you use, you will put on weight.

Oranges and other citrus fruit contain lots of vitamin C, which has many benefits including boosting the body's immune system.

Fish are a good source of proteins.

It is important to eat plenty of vegetables as part of a balanced diet. Green vegetables provide a number of vitamins, including A, E and K. They also provide calcium and iron.

CONTENTS

Why we need food

You will find out:
- Why we need food
- What the functions of carbohydrates, proteins and fats are

Fat, obese or just big?

Sumo is an ancient Japanese sport. As part of their training, sumo wrestlers eat about ten times the normal daily amount of food. Their main meal each day consists of chanko nabe. This is a high-energy stew made from seaweed, chicken, fish and vegetables. Sumo wrestlers can weigh anywhere between 150 kg and 230 kg! The bigger they are, the better their chances are of winning fights. So big is good!

FIGURE 1: Are these sumo wrestlers fat, obese, or just big?

Why food?

Food contains **nutrients** – chemical compounds such as **proteins**, **fats**, **carbohydrates**, **vitamins** or **minerals** – which your body needs. There are seven major **food groups** (see table 1).

Your body needs a variety of these nutrients to have a balanced diet. Food is necessary for four main reasons:

- for energy (**respiration**) ■ for **growth** ■ for **repair** ■ for health.

For energy: You need nutrients to provide energy for **movement**. Respiration is the reaction that releases energy from food:

food + oxygen → carbon dioxide + water + energy

Different nutrients give you different amounts of energy (see table 2). The four food groups not included in the table do not give you energy.

More active people use up more energy. Although fats contain more energy per gram than any other food group, you tend to get most energy from carbohydrates. This is because carbohydrates are easier to digest than fats or proteins. Someone doing heavy work might need as much as 20 000 kJ of energy every day, whereas someone doing light office work could use less than half of this.

Growth and repair: Many cells only live for a few days or weeks. As they wear out, get damaged or die, they have to be replaced. New cells are made from the chemicals you eat. In this way, your body tissues are kept in top working order.

Food group	Good sources
carbohydrates	bread, potatoes, pasta, rice
proteins	lean meat, fish, pulses
fats	butter, cheese
vitamins	fresh fruit
minerals	meat, eggs, milk, fresh fruit and vegetables
water	drinks
fibre	vegetables, pulses, nuts

TABLE 1: The seven major food groups.

Nutrient	Energy content (kJ/g)
carbohydrate	16
protein	17
fat	38

TABLE 2: Energy content of various nutrients.

Health: To be healthy you need a 'balanced diet'. This would contain a range of different foods depending on your age, gender and levels of activity. You can learn more about this on pages 36–37.

> ## ■ QUESTIONS ■
>
> 1 Why does your body need food?
> 2 Look at table 1. For each food group give another example of a food that is not listed in the table.
> 3 What is a balanced diet and what does it depend on?
> 4 Explain why you would expect an office worker to use less energy than a labourer.

Carbohydrates

These are sugary and starchy foods and your body's main source of energy. If you eat too many, your body will convert them into fat, which is stored under the skin.

Fats

There are two types of fats. Table 3 shows the differences. Fats provide:

- Insulation (you need some fat to keep warm).
- Energy (fats contain twice as much energy as proteins and carbohydrates).
- Protection (fats protect some of your organs, e.g. kidneys).
- Source of vitamins (vitamins A, D, E and K are fat-soluble).

Type	Source	Difference	Danger to our health?
saturated fat	meat (animal fat)	no double bonds between atoms	Yes, it can stick to the insides of blood vessels and gradually block them
unsaturated fat	vegetables (plant fat)	lots of double bonds between atoms	No, they do not stick to blood vessels

TABLE 3: Differences between saturated and unsaturated fats.

Proteins

Your body uses proteins for growth and for replacing damaged and worn-out cells. Your digestive system breaks proteins down into amino acids. These are absorbed into the blood, taken to parts of your body that need them and reassembled into the required proteins.

Type of food	Carbohydrates (g per 100 g)	Proteins (g per 100 g)	Fats (g per 100 g)	Energy content (kj per 100 g)
Meat and fish				
roast chicken	0	24.8	5.4	621
beef sausages	11.7	9.6	24.1	1242
cod	7.5	19.6	10.3	834
Dairy produce				
cheese	0	25.4	34.5	1708
whole milk	4.8	3.3	3.8	274
Bread and cakes				
wholemeal bread	46.7	9.6	3.1	1025
fruit cake	55.0	4.6	15.9	1546
Fruit and vegetables				
lettuce	1.2	1.0	0	36
tomatoes	2.4	0.8	0	52
potatoes	19.7	1.4	0	339

TABLE 4: Nutrient and energy contents of various foods.

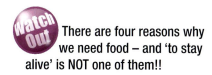 There are four reasons why we need food – and 'to stay alive' is NOT one of them!!

Good fat; bad fat?

Eating a lot of saturated fats has been linked to an increased risk of vascular disease and heart attacks. Saturated fats generally come from animals. They include lard, butter, cheese and whole milk and also the white fat found in red meat and under the skin of chicken.

Unsaturated fats are considered to be healthier. They are found in vegetable oils, like olive oil, and oily fish such as sardines and mackerel.

A balanced diet should contain both saturated and unsaturated fats.

FIGURE 2: Olive oil contains unsaturated fats.

QUESTIONS

6 You are a doctor. One of your patients has had a heart attack. When you ask him about his diet, you are told that he eats:

- lots of fried food, cooked in lard
- full cooked breakfasts (bacon, eggs, sausages, etc.)
- cod and chips and other 'fast food'
- no green vegetables.

Write a letter to your patient giving him specific advice about changing his diet.

QUESTIONS

5 What is the energy content of the following meal:

- 100 g of roast chicken
- 150 g of potatoes
- 50 g of lettuce
- 50 g of tomatoes.

...nutrients ...proteins ...repair ...respiration ...vitamins

Vitamins

You will find out:
- What vitamins are
- The jobs that vitamins A, B, D, K and C do for the human body
- The effects of vitamin deficiencies on the human body

Is preserved food healthy?

Before we had fridges, making pickles and chutneys was a common way of preserving fruit and vegetables for the winter. Cooking these foods kills bacteria and other microorganisms that cause food to go 'off'. Sadly the process also destroys many of the **vitamins** in the food. Pickles and chutneys might taste nice, but are they healthy?

FIGURE 1: Do you think that pickles like these are healthy?

What are vitamins?

Vitamins are complicated chemicals that you need for healthy growth and development, but only in tiny amounts. If you lack a particular vitamin, you will develop a **deficiency disease**. Dieticians and food scientists study foods. They tell you what to eat as part of a healthy, balanced diet.

Vitamin	Source	Function	Symptoms of deficiency
A	• fish liver oil • dairy products • carrots • watercress	• healthy eyesight • keeps mucus membranes free from infection	• poor vision (not able to see in dim light) • dry skin • dry mucus membranes
B1	• yeast • brown rice • beans • nuts	• releases energy from carbohydrates • healthy nerves	• anaemia • mouth sores • nerve cell degeneration
C	• citrus fruits (e.g. oranges and lemons) • tomatoes • red and green peppers • spinach	• stimulates the immune system (helps the body to fight disease) • absorption of iron (prevents anaemia) • maintenance of skin and the linings of the digestive system	• bleeding gums • cuts will not heal (symptoms of **scurvy**) • weak blood vessels
D	• fish liver oil • dairy products • egg yolk	• absorption of calcium and phosphorus for healthy teeth and bones	• weak bones (these may become deformed due to excess body weight – a condition called **rickets**) • weak teeth
K	• spinach • cabbage • Brussels sprouts	• helps blood to clot	• blood clots more slowly or not at all

TABLE 1: Vitamins, where you can get them and what might happen if you don't!

FIGURE 2: Foods containing vitamins must be part of a balanced diet.

QUESTIONS

1. What are vitamins?
2. How do dieticians help you?
3. Cheese and watercress are a good source of which vitamin?
4. What symptoms are you likely to develop if you lack vitamin C?

...deficiency disease   ...rickets

Vitamin C

Vitamin C is also known as ascorbic acid. A lack of vitamin C causes the deficiency disease scurvy. When someone suffers from scurvy they could show any or all of the following symptoms:

- very fragile blood capillaries
- bruising and bleeding
- internal bleeding
- weakness and tiredness
- swollen gums
- loss of teeth.

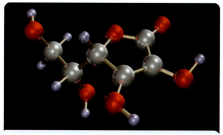

FIGURE 3: A vitamin C molecule.

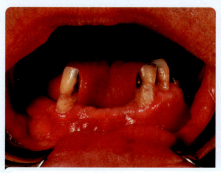 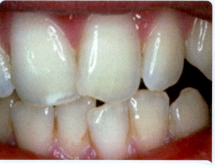

FIGURE 4: Which of these two mouths show the symptoms of scurvy?

British sailors – 'limeys'

Two hundred years ago, British sailors often showed signs of scurvy, especially if they were on very long voyages. Their diet lacked fresh fruit and vegetables. The naval doctor, James Lind (1716–1794) found that if he gave sailors lime juice (a citrus fruit), they would not get scurvy. This is why British sailors were called 'limeys'.

A chemical test for vitamin C

DCPIP is a very dark blue liquid that loses its colour when added to vitamin C. (Dichlorophenolindophenol is the proper name for DCPIP, so it's not too surprising that we shorten it!)

A food technologist read that vitamin C is destroyed by heat. She carried out the following experiment:

- She extracted the juice of two limes.
- She put 1 cm³ of lime juice into each of 11 test tubes.
- She kept each tube at a different temperature for 10 minutes.
- She put 1 cm³ of DCPIP into 11 other test tubes.
- She then counted how many drops of lime juice it took to decolorise the DCPIP.

Here are the results:

Temperature of lime juice/°C	0	10	20	30	40	50	60	70	80	90	100
Number of drops of lime juice needed to decolorise the DCPIP	2	2	2	2	2	3	4	7	15	25	47

TABLE 2: Results of the vitamin C and temperature experiment.

QUESTIONS

5 List **three** symptoms of scurvy.
6 Why were British sailors called 'limeys'?
7 Draw a line graph of the results in table 2.
8 Do these results support the idea that heat destroys vitamin C? Explain your answer.

Rickets and vitamin D

Rickets is caused by a lack of vitamin D and causes softening and weakening of the bones. A typical sign of rickets is 'bowed' legs. We get vitamin D in two ways:

- in the food we eat (see table 1)
- it is produced by our skin when it is exposed to sunlight.

Rickets can be prevented by taking in sufficient calcium and phosphorus in the diet, together with exposure to sunlight. Many dermatologists (doctors who deal with skin diseases) recommend taking vitamin D tablets in preference to unprotected sunbathing.

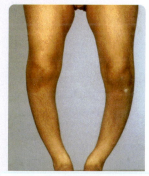

FIGURE 5: Bowed legs of someone suffering from rickets.

QUESTIONS

9 Suggest **two** foods that would help prevent someone from developing rickets.
10 There is a form of rickets that is inherited. In your group, discuss how you could establish if a child's rickets is caused by poor diet or inheritance.
11 Why would a dermatologist recommend taking vitamin D tablets?

...scurvy   ...vitamins

Minerals

You will find out:
- Why the human body needs iron, calcium, phosphorus and zinc
- About foods that contain these minerals

Budgies need minerals too

Cuttlefish are animals similar to squid. They grow up to about 25 cm long. They live in the seas around southern England as well as the Mediterranean. Budgie owners give cuttlefish bones to their birds. The budgies peck at the bone, which helps to keep their beaks trim and sharp. It also supplies them with the **calcium** they need for healthy bones. What about you? How do you get the **minerals** you need to stay healthy?

FIGURE 1: What is this budgie getting from the cuttlefish bone?

What are minerals?

Minerals (sometimes called essential minerals or mineral salts) are chemicals that you need for healthy growth and development. You only need small amounts to keep healthy. If you lack a particular mineral, you will become ill. A **dietician** can tell you what to eat as part of a healthy, balanced diet.

Mineral	Source	Function	Symptoms of deficiency
Iron	• red meat (e.g. beef and lamb) and liver • real chocolate • beans and nuts	• makes haemoglobin in red blood cells • some enzymes need it to work properly	• anaemia
Calcium	• milk and dairy products (except butter) • beans • nuts	• healthy development of strong bones and teeth	• stunted growth • poor teeth • poor bones
Phosphorus	• red meat • milk and dairy products • cereals	• aids release of energy from food • development of healthy bones and teeth	• liver disease • rickets
Zinc	• meat • cereals • seafood	• for enzyme action • helps wounds to heal • prevents eyesight problems in old age	• poor physical performance • nerves do not work properly • loss of taste and smell • eyesight problems in old age

TABLE 1: Minerals, where you can get them and what happens if you don't!

QUESTIONS

1. What are minerals?
2. Why do you need calcium?
3. What effect does a diet lacking in zinc have on your body?
4. Why does your body need phosphorus?

How do these minerals help us?

Iron and blood

An adult human body contains between 2.3 and 3.8 g of iron. Most of this is found in the haemoglobin of red blood cells and is involved in oxygen transport.

The human body requires different amounts of iron in the diet, depending on age and sex. Table 2 shows how much iron is needed in relation to age.

Age range	Iron/mg/day males		Iron/mg/day males/females		Iron/mg/day females
0–3 months			1.7		
4–6 months			4.3		
7–12 months			7.8		
1–3 years			6.9		
4–6 years			6.1		
7–10 years			8.7		
11–18 years	11.3				14.8
19–50 years	8.7				14.8
50+ years	8.7				8.7

TABLE 2: Daily iron requirements.

Calcium and phosphorus

As a baby develops in its mother's uterus, its bones are soft. After birth, for the bones to become hard (a process called calcification), the child must have a good supply of calcium and phosphorus. This normally comes in the form of calcium phosphate and calcium carbonate, both found in milk. Vitamin D is needed to absorb these. A similar process happens to make teeth hard.

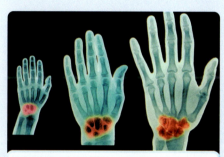
FIGURE 2: What differences can you see in these bones from (a) a 2-year-old child, (b) a 7-year-old child and (c) an adult?

Zinc – too much of a good thing

Dieticians have carried out studies and found that if your diet contains too much zinc, you might suffer from stomach and intestinal cramps, nausea and anaemia.

Age group	Recommended daily intake/mg
Infant	5
1–10 years	10
Adult female	12
Adult male	15
Pregnant female	15

TABLE 3: Zinc intake recommended by the World Health Organization

How much do you need?

Age group	Daily calcium requirements in mg
Birth to 6 months	210
6–12 months	270
1–3 years	500
4–8 years	800
9–18 years	1300
19–50 years	1000
50+ years	1200

TABLE 4: Daily calcium requirements.

Osteoporosis is a condition that many older people develop. It results in their bones breaking more easily. It is caused by a lack of calcium and other minerals found in bones.

QUESTIONS

9 Present the data in table 4 as a graph.

10 Why should people over the age of about 50 increase their daily calcium intake?

11 You have an elderly relative (perhaps a grandparent). Write a letter to them advising them about the dangers of a lack of calcium in their diet.

QUESTIONS

5 Suggest why babies need less iron in their daily diet than adults.

6 Suggest why males between the ages of 11 and 50 need less iron than females of the same age.

7 Why do babies and young children need a good supply of calcium and phosphorus?

8 Why does the daily zinc requirement change with age?

...minerals ..phosphorus ...zinc

Healthy eating

You will find out:
- About daily energy requirements
- About the importance of fibre for health
- Why it is important to have a healthy diet
- About the effect of marketing on lifestyle and health

Fat can be fatal

Carol Yager died of kidney failure in 1994. She was 34 years old and weighed about 660 kg at the time of her death. She had been overweight since childhood. When she lived her muscles were not strong enough to lift her. Her bones would have broken under the strain. Could she have avoided this? Would a healthy diet have helped her?

Energy in; energy out!

The amount of energy that you need depends on your:
- age
- sex
- what you do.

A lot of the energy you need comes from the sugars (carbohydrates) and fats you eat. If your **energy intake** is more than you need, you are likely to put on weight. And if you eat less than you require, you are likely to lose weight.

	Approximate daily energy requirements/kJ	
	Female	**Male**
7-year-old	8400	8400
14–15-year-old	9800	12 400
Adult office worker	9900	11 200
Adult builder	13 000	15 200
Pregnant woman	10 100	–
Breast-feeding woman	11 400	–

TABLE 1: Approximate daily energy requirements.

How important is fibre?

Dietary **fibre** is important for five main reasons:
- It adds bulk to your food, giving intestines something to push against as they move food along.
- It prevents constipation.
- It is believed to prevent cancer of the large intestine.
- It is believed to lower blood cholesterol.
- It absorbs poisonous waste during digestion.

Fibre comes from eating fruit and vegetables, so remember your 'five a day'!

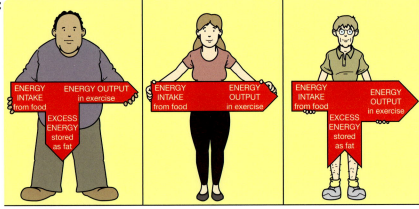

Fatter person   Average person   Thinner person

FIGURE 1: What is your energy intake like?

QUESTIONS

1 What does your daily energy intake depend on?
2 How does daily energy intake affect your weight?
3 Explain why 'five a day' (five portions of fruit and/or vegetables) is important for health.

Remember your 'five a day'!

Life in the fast lane

Life in the 21st century can be fast and stressful. Your **lifestyle** could mean that there just is not enough time to rest and reflect on what is going on around you. This could mean that you take shortcuts with your health. Ask yourself – do you pay attention to the following:

- Diet – do you have a balanced diet or are you influenced by the **marketing** of **fast foods**?
- Exercise – are you active or a 'couch potato'?
- Rest – do you get enough sleep, or are you always tired?

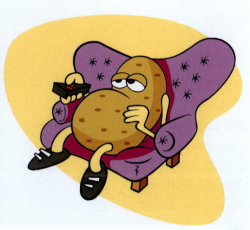

FIGURE 2: Do you play sport ... or ...are you a couch potato?

Health risks related to diet

- Saturated fat: found in animal products like meat and dairy products. Your liver converts saturated fats into cholesterol. Cholesterol can block blood vessels and increase the risk of heart disease.
- Salt: adds flavour to the food you eat. But too much salt can result in high blood pressure. Doctors and scientists recommend a maximum of 6 g a day. Many people eat much more than 6 g, even though your body only needs about 1 g each day.

The health risks of eating too much saturated fat, sugar and salt include:

- heart disease
- diabetes
- high blood pressure.

QUESTIONS

4 What is meant by 'lifestyle'?

5 Explain the effect of exercise on your health.

6 Explain why saturated fats are bad for your health.

7 Write down **three** things that you could do to have a better, healthier, lifestyle.

Fat rats: genes and/or greed?

At the National Institute of Nutrition in India, scientists have some fat rats. The biggest of these weighs in at a stunning 1.4 kg, four times the mean weight of a normal rat. They eat four times the normal amount of food each day, so it is hardly surprising they are so big. The scientists have found that as the rats grow and become obese, they develop conditions such as tumours and cataracts. All were infertile and their life expectancy was cut to about 18 months – 50% of normal life expectancy. A gene has been found that controls the production of the hormone leptin. This is an appetite suppressor, released by fat cells. It makes you want to eat less and is used in an anti-obesity drug. Although these rats have high levels of leptin, they still put on lots of weight.

FIGURE 3: Normal rat on the right and obese rat on the left.

QUESTIONS

8 What is the life expectancy of a normal rat?

9 What is the weight of a normal rat?

10 Suggest why the fat rats ate so much and put on weight, in spite of having the leptin-producing gene.

11 Write down as many reasons as you can why scientists should not use rats in experiments.

...lifestyle ...marketing

As clear as juice?

INVESTIGATION

One of the growth areas in food sales in recent years has been cloudy apple juices. At one time, all mass-produced apple juice was clear. Food manufacturers assumed this was what the public would buy. Now, however, several brands of cloudy apple juice are available alongside the clear ones, so that customers have a choice.

Rachel is interested in this because she and her friends have different points of view. Rachel thinks that cloudy apple juice is great and always prefers it to clear, but Gary and Colin disagree. Colin thinks that, in fact, very few people like cloudy juice. They decide that this is a good idea for an investigation.

Here is Rachel's report:
I decided to study the popularity of cloudy apple juice because this is the kind of investigation that a food scientist might be involved with. Apple juice isn't just cloudy or clear. There are different degrees of cloudiness. Our investigation is about how the cloudiness affects the popularity of the juice. This information would be very useful to a food manufacturer so that they could decide whether to market a cloudy apple juice and how cloudy it should be.

The production process includes filtration of the apple juice, and the manufacturer can decide to what extent the juice is filtered. Less filtration means more solids in suspension and this produces a cloudier juice.

3A.1 Rachel has researched and explained the significance of the application that she is going to investigate and has clearly explained its relevance to food processing.

Rachel's plan for the investigation is shown below:

We tested six apple juices, three cloudy and three clear. The cloudiness we measured as clarity and we did this by shining a light through it and looking to see how clear it was. We made a judgement by comparing it with water and with milk. The more light gets through the greater the clarity of the juice.

We had to make sure when we tested the apple juices for clarity that it was a fair test. The light had to be shone through the same size container of juice. We then gave it a mark for clarity on a scale of 1–10 where water has a clarity of 10 and milk a clarity of 1. We measured the clarity of each of the apple juices and then asked a number of people to try each of the juices and to give them a score out of ten. We then looked at the scores to see if there was any pattern with the clarity.

2B.1 Rachel has produced a plan for the investigation, which is detailed enough to be followed by another person and clearly shows how the clarity is to be tested fairly. To improve her mark, Rachel could produce a more detailed plan for the investigation. What is the actual sequence of steps?

As clear as juice?

STUDENT'S COMMENTARY

As we were asking people to taste the juice, we carried out that part of the investigation in the food technology room using utensils kept clean for that purpose. We completed a risk assessment form given to us by our teacher.

Risk Assessment Form

DESCRIBE THE INVESTIGATION

We are going to measure how cloudy different kinds of apple juice are by shining a light through them and comparing the amount that gets through with water and with milk. We are also going to get people to taste and talk about the flavour of the apple juices.

WHAT ARE THE HAZARDS?

I think that there are two hazards with this experiment. One is that we are having to look at light travelling through a liquid and if the light is bright and was on the opposite side of the liquid to us, the light might travel straight into our eyes. The other is that some of the apple juice might get contaminated by chemicals.

WHAT ARE THE RISKS?

Shining a light in your eyes might damage the eye and temporarily affect your vision. Contaminated apple juice could cause poisoning, which can be serious.

HOW CAN THE RISK BE CONTROLLED?

We will set the equipment up so that we are viewing the liquids from the side when light is being shone through them.

We will do the tasting of the apple juice in a Food Technology room and using the rules that go with food: washing hands before and after, washing containers after use, nothing with hand to mouth, etc.

WHAT IS THE REMAINING RISK?

Very low as long as we follow the rules.

2B.2 Rachel has carried out a risk assessment, but the form she used had some guidelines. She could improve her mark by carrying out the risk assessment more independently.

The evidence

Juice	Description	Clarity	Student rating (average) on a scale of 0–10
A	Clear	9	7.6
B	Clear	9	7.8
C	Clear	8	6.2
D	Slightly cloudy	6	4.4
E	Cloudy	3	7.1
F	Very cloudy	2	3.9

2C.1 Rachel has selected the appropriate equipment for the investigation with a little guidance from her teacher and has used it correctly and safely to carry out the plan to collect and record data accurately. To improve her work, Rachel could arrange to repeat her measurements; although the student ratings were an average of a number of opinions, the clarity readings were only taken once each.

What it means

At first it was difficult to see what these results show, because it seemed to be that the cloudier the juice, the less popular it was; but Juice E was nearly as popular as Juices A and B and it was much cloudier. But then we thought about what people had said during the tasting, and those people who did like cloudy apple juice really liked Juice E.

If you were to make only one juice, you would make it a clear one; but if you were to make two, you would make a clear one and also a cloudy one like Juice E.

2D.1 Rachel has used the information collected from her investigation to draw some conclusions. She has thought carefully about what the results show and has presented some interesting ideas based on these, but needs to present more evidence to support the conclusions in detail.

How I might improve the investigation

I think that this investigation went very well and the results showed an interesting pattern, which I think we explained well. However, we don't really know why people preferred the juices that they did. We assumed it was because they were more or less cloudy, but people choose juices for different reasons and it could be that some people don't care what it looks like but just go by the taste.

If we did this again, we might ask people to just look at the juices and pick which one they thought looked nicest.

We didn't do anything on price and I know that cloudy apple juices cost more, and that might affect what people choose as well.

3E.1 Rachel has evaluated her investigation and has made a suggestion as to how to improve the method. She has made some good points about the limitations of her method and has pointed out that their assumption that preference is based on appearance is not a safe one.

She hasn't, however, been very clear about how they would collect more useful data, and she would have been awarded more marks if she had made it clear how the information gathered could be used by people involved in food manufacturing.

Food additives

You will find out:
- Why we add food additives to our food
- What 'E' numbers are
- What the advantages and disadvantages are of food additives

Food or chemicals?

Some of the ingredients listed on this packet of sweets make them taste nice! But do they affect you in other ways? E104, E122, E110, E127 and E132 are all known to cause hyperactivity. E330 causes intestinal upsets. Only E322 is *thought* to be safe! So why are additives put in the food that we eat?

Ingredients: Glucose Syrup · Sugar · Strawberry, Blackcurrant, Lemon, Orange, Apple Juices (4.4%) · Hydrogenated Vegetable Oil · Citric Acid E330 · Gelatine · Egg White · Flavourings · Colours E104 E122 E110 E127 E132 E142 · Emulsifier E322.

FIGURE 1: Do you think that all these ingredients are safe?

Why additives?

Food manufacturers use **food additives** for three main reasons:
- to improve the **taste** of food
- to increase its **shelf life**
- to improve its **appearance** (to make it look nicer).

E numbers

Every legal food additive has an **E number**. This means that it has been tested to establish that it is safe to use. All E-numbered additives have been approved for use throughout the European Union.

Type of additive	What they do	Example	E number	A food it is added to
Antioxidants	Make food last longer, increases shelf life.	Vitamin C (ascorbic acid)	E300	Often added to foods containing fat or oil, e.g. pies, mayonnaise
Flavourings	Include flavours and flavour enhancers. These 'bring out' the flavour of some foods.	Monosodium glutamate (MSG)	E621	Processed foods such as soups and sausages
Colourings	Make food colourful, either because the food has lost its natural colour during processing or because manufacturers think it will look nice.	Tartrazine	E102	Yellow colour found in orange squash and other yellow foods
Preservatives	Stop food 'going off' and make it last longer.	Benzoic acid	E210	Jam, preserved fruit, fruit juice
Sweeteners	Alternative to sugar. They have a lower energy content and are often much sweeter than sugar.	Aspartame	E951	Fizzy drinks
Thickeners	Give 'body' to food.	Starch (there are a number of different types)	E numbers between E1401 and E1451.	Thick, processed foods like soups

TABLE 1: Food additives.

QUESTIONS

1. Why do food manufacturers use food additives?
2. What is an E number?
3. What does tartrazine do?
4. Suggest **two** reasons why colourings are added to food.

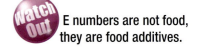

E numbers are not food, they are food additives.

Hyperactivity and food additives

In Britain there are over 500 different foods and drinks intended for children. It is now believed that lots of these snacks and drinks are responsible for some children's **hyperactive behaviour**. Research scientists tested the effect of five commonly used additives on nearly 300 3-year-olds. For their study, the scientists made a drink containing the additives listed in table 2 at levels similar to those found in food.

E number	Name	What it does
E102	Tartrazine	yellow colour
E110	Sunset yellow	yellow colour
E122	Carmoisine	red colour
E124	Ponceau 4R	red colour
E211	Sodium benzoate	preservative

TABLE 2: Food additives used in the study.

The children were given a cup full of the drink. Many parents recorded significant changes in their children's behaviour. A spokesperson from the research team said: "Over 200 children's foods and drinks contain at least one of the additives used in the study." She continued: "We feel that these findings support the call to ban the use of these additives in children's foods and drinks."

FIGURE 2: Active or hyperactive: have these children had some E102?

FIGURE 3: Sweets are often brightly coloured with artificial additives, but are these colours any brighter than the natural ones from plants?

QUESTIONS

5 List **three** foods/drinks that are intended for children.

6 What does 'hyperactive' mean?

7 How would the children's behaviour have changed after taking the drink?

8 Do you think that the additives listed in table 2 should be removed from children's snacks and drinks? Explain your answer.

Food additives affect eyesight

FIGURE 4: Is takeaway food a good idea? See what you think.

In 2002 Japanese food scientists showed that high levels of MSG can damage parts of the eyes of laboratory rats. MSG is used in the production of Oriental and processed foods. Rats fed on high levels of MSG suffered from loss of vision and developed abnormal retinas (the part of the eye that is light-sensitive).

Group of rats	% of MSG in diet	Effect
1	20	much thinner retina poor vision in natural light
2	10	slightly thinner retina
3	0	no effect

TABLE 3: Effect of MSG on eyesight of rats.

The lead Japanese researcher said: "Lesser amounts of MSG should be OK, though the exact quantities are not known." But scientists in Britain were sceptical. One was quoted as saying: "If you have the odd takeaway, I shouldn't worry."

QUESTIONS

9 What does 'sceptical' mean?

10 Why was group 3 included in the investigation?

11 Design an experiment to show exactly how much MSG has an adverse effect on rat eyes.

Food tests

You will find out:
- That the food we eat often contains more than one nutrient
- How to carry out chemical tests on food for starch, fat, protein, reducing sugar and acidity
- How to interpret the information on food labels

Are you intolerant?

Only about 2% of the population show food intolerance. This happens when your body reacts to particular food ingredients. Some people can't drink cow's milk; they get wind, stomach cramps or even diarrhoea. Many are not able to eat nuts; their breathing is affected. Nuts can even cause anaphylactic shock. Do you have to be careful about what you eat? Do you check food labels?

FIGURE 1: If you have an intolerance to nuts, these could kill you.

What do food labels tell you?

Have you ever wondered where the information on a **food label** comes from? A **food analyst** is a scientist who tests foods for their content. This means that when food manufacturers label their products the information we see is accurate. The food analysts carry out simple chemical tests for:

- **starch** ■ **reducing sugar** (**glucose**) ■ **fat** ■ **protein** ■ **acidity**.

Starch

- Place a few drops of starch solution in a well of a 'spotting tile'.
- Add 1–2 drops of orange-coloured iodine solution.
- It will turn a blue/black colour.
- This is a positive result for starch.
- Test a range of foods with iodine to see if they contain starch.

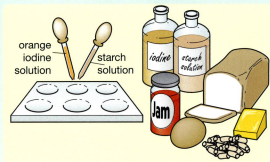

FIGURE 2: Chemical test for starch.

Reducing sugar (glucose)

- Pour 1–2 cm^3 of glucose into a test tube.
- Add 1–2 cm^3 of blue Benedict's solution.
- Heat the test tube in a water bath.
- It will turn an orangey-brown colour.
- This is a positive result for reducing sugar.
- Test a range of foods with Benedict's solution to see if they contain glucose.

FIGURE 3: Chemical test for reducing sugar (glucose).

Fat

- Pour 1–2 cm^3 of cooking oil into a test tube.
- Add about 4 cm^3 of clear, colourless ethanol.
- Put a stopper in the tube and shake it.
- Let the mixture settle for a few seconds.
- Carefully pour off the top 2 cm^3 into a clean test tube.
- Add 2 cm^3 of water, stopper the tube and shake it.
- It will turn white, which is a positive result for fat.
- Test a range of foods to see if they contain fat.

FIGURE 4: Chemical test for fat.

Protein

- Pour 2 cm³ of egg albumen solution (rich in protein) into a test tube.
- Add 2 cm³ of clear, colourless sodium hydroxide solution.
- Put a stopper in the tube and shake it.
- Now add 2–3 drops of blue copper sulfate solution.
- It will turn a pale violet colour, which is a positive result for protein.
- Test a range of foods to see if they contain protein.

Acidity

- Shake a sample of food up with some water.
- Dip a piece of litmus paper into it.
- Red means that it is acidic and blue means that it is alkaline.

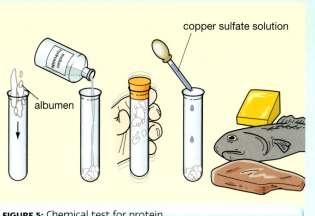

copper sulfate solution

albumen

FIGURE 5: Chemical test for protein.

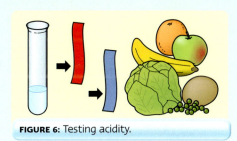

FIGURE 6: Testing acidity.

By law, food manufacturers have to give consumers the following information about their food:

- **sell-by date**
- quantities of **nutrients**
- energy values of the nutrients
- other components of the food such as colourings and flavourings (these are called **food additives** and you have learnt about them on pages 42–43).

It is very important to know what is in the food you eat. Food labelling can help you decide what to eat as part of a healthy and balanced diet.

Analysing nutritional information

Oatcakes are biscuits that are often eaten with cheese. Here is the nutritional information from a packet of oatcakes:

Typical values	Per oatcake	Per 100 g
energy	239 kJ	1890 kJ
protein	1.3 g	10.4 g
carbohydrate: sugars	0.3 g	2.5 g
carbohydrate: starch	6.8 g	53.9 g
fats	2.6 g	20.4 g
fibre	0.8 g	6.7 g
salt	0.2 g	1.4 g
water	0.6 g	???

QUESTIONS

1. What does a food analyst do?
2. How can you tell if a sample of food contains starch?
3. What would you use Benedict's solution for?
4. How would you know if a sample of food does not contain any glucose?
5. Whole milk contains fat. Why is the fat test shown above not very useful in this case?
6. Write a sentence or short paragraph to describe how you would test a food sample for protein.
7. What is a sell-by date and why is it important?
8. Why is it important to know the things that are in the food you eat?

QUESTIONS

9. How many oatcakes are there in 100 g?
10. Estimate how much water there is in 100 g of oatcakes. Explain how you got your answer.
11. Draw a block graph of the mass of nutrients per 100 g of oatcakes.
12. Some doctors recommend that each day we should have 6 g of salt. How many oatcakes would provide you with your daily recommended amount of salt?

Food analysis

You will find out:
- How to measure the amount of moisture in food
- How much suspended matter there is in liquid food
- About the acidity of food
- About the iron content of food

What food contains

Food scientists and biochemists analyse food to see what it contains. They carry out laboratory tests using various pieces of apparatus. It is important to know about the food you eat to ensure that it contains the things you need to be healthy. Do you know what the food you eat contains?

How much water is there in food?

The food you eat contains water. Some foods, like fruit and vegetables, are obviously very wet. But even apparently dry things, like biscuits, contain water. The following method can be used to calculate the water content:

- Take a biscuit and weigh it.
- Place it on a heat-proof dish.
- Put it in an oven set at 110 °C for 24 hours.
- Re-weigh it.
- The difference is the water content.
- Calculate the percentage of water.

  Example:

  Mass of biscuit in g   8.3

  Mass of dried biscuit in g   7.4

  Difference in g   0.9

So the percentage of water in this biscuit is: $\frac{0.9}{8.3} \times 100 = 10.8\%$

FIGURE 1: How to find the water content of a biscuit.

Suspended matter in liquid food

Many liquid foods have got 'bits' in, e.g. fresh orange juice and chicken noodle soup. The 'bits' are called **suspended matter**. Try this:

- Measure out 100 cm³ of freshly squeezed orange juice (with bits).
- Filter it.
- Examine the filter paper.
- Repeat this procedure with different fruit juices and compare your results.

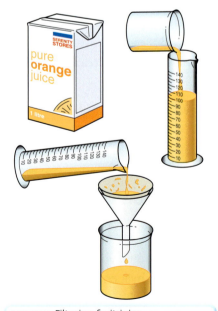

FIGURE 2: Filtering fruit juice.

> **QUESTIONS**
>
> 1 Cream-crackers are very dry, and contain very little water. The mass of a cream-cracker is 4.7 g. After 24 hours in an oven it lost 0.3 g. What is the percentage of water in this cracker?
>
> 2 How could you work out the dry mass of the suspended matter in a cup of vegetable soup?

...Reference Nutritional Intake (RNI)

Iron in food supplements

Iron is an important mineral found in various foods. You can also get all the iron you need by taking iron tablets. The iron can be extracted from food by boiling with water or dilute acid. A chemical that reacts with the dissolved iron to give a coloured solution is added to the extract. The intensity of the colour depends on how much iron is present. The amount of iron can be estimated by comparing the colour formed with standard solutions of iron treated in the same way.

How much acid is in your food?

Generally we like the sharp taste of acid food. Oranges and lemons have a sharp taste because of the acid they contain. But how much acid is there in them?

Try this investigation, called a **titration**, to find out how much acid – actually it's ascorbic acid, or vitamin C – there is in a tomato:

- Weigh the whole tomato and write down the weight.
- Thoroughly grind up 1 g of the tomato in 5 cm^3 of water – use a pestle and mortar.
- Filter the mixture to get a clear solution – this is what you will now use.
- Take 1 cm^3 of the liquid and put it in a test tube.
- Place the test tube under a burette containing 0.1% DCPIP solution and add it, drop by drop, to the tomato liquid in the test tube (there is information about DCPIP on page 33).
- Carry on adding the DCPIP until its dark blue colour disappears completely (the DCPIP is said to decolorise).
- Write down the volume of DCPIP you used.

This volume is equivalent to the amount of acid in the tomato.

You can now work out how much acid there is. This is how to do it:

Say your 1 cm^3 of tomato extract needed 1.5 cm^3 of 0.1% DCPIP; as each cm^3 of DCPIP contains 0.001 g, the 1 cm^3 of tomato extract will contain 0.0015 g of ascorbic acid.

This means that your original 1 g of tomato will have contained 0.0015 g x 5 (volume of water you used) = 0.0075 g

You can then multiply this answer by the total mass of the whole tomato. This will give you the total amount of vitamin C in the tomato.

Very acidic foods, like lemons, contain lots of acid. This makes the DCPIP turn pink, so look for a pink colour rather than dark blue.

FIGURE 3: In this titration, the DCPIP has just turned pink. What does this mean?

QUESTIONS

3   Why is it important to have vitamin C in your diet?

4   5 g of fresh strawberry decolorises 2 cm^3 of 0.1% DCPIP. How much vitamin C is there in a 35 g strawberry?

Food labels

By law, food manufacturers have to say what is in the food you buy. The **Reference Nutritional Intake** (**RNI**) represents enough or more than enough to meet your daily needs for nutrients. Vitamins are chemical compounds that your body cannot make, so they have to be taken in with your food.

Age range	Vitamin C/mg/day
0–3 months	25
4–6 months	25
7–9 months	25
10–12 months	25
1–3 years	30
4–6 years	30
7–10 years	30
11–14 years	35
15–18 years	40
19–50 years	40
50+ years	40

TABLE 1: Daily vitamin C RNI.

Here are the vitamin C contents of various foods:

Food/100 g	Vitamin C content /mg
roast lamb	0
peas	14
chips	15
tinned peaches	4
custard	0

TABLE 2: Vitamin C content of some foods.

QUESTIONS

5   Draw an appropriate graph of the daily vitamin C RNI figures.

6   What mass of chips would an average 35-year-old have to eat to get the daily RNI?

7   Explain why fresh peaches have a vitamin C content that is much higher than tinned peaches.

Microorganisms and food production

You will find out:
- How microorganisms are used in food production
- What microbiologists do

Beer and microbes

Beer is one of the oldest drinks in the world. Over 5000 years ago, the Sumerians, who lived in what is now Iraq, had recipes for it. Even the ancient Egyptians brewed it. The sugar in germinating seeds, like barley, is fermented by yeast. Enzymes in yeast convert the sugars into alcohol. Every culture in the world uses microbes to make food and alcohol.

What are microorganisms?

Most people associate **microorganisms** with germs – and germs mean disease! But many microorganisms are useful to us. They are used to produce some foods and drinks, for example:

- yoghurt   **bacteria**
- cheese   bacteria (and sometimes **fungi**)
- beer   **yeast**
- wine   yeast
- bread   yeast

Bacteria

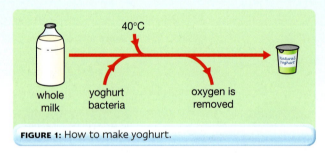

FIGURE 1: How to make yoghurt.

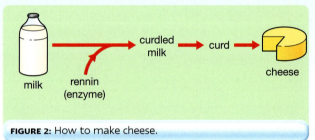

FIGURE 2: How to make cheese.

Some cheeses, like Stilton and Danish Blue, have had a fungus added to them. This gives them their marbled blue appearance and their characteristic taste.

Yeast

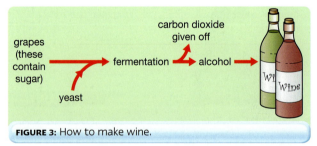

FIGURE 3: How to make wine.

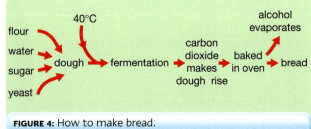

FIGURE 4: How to make bread.

QUESTIONS

1 What does the word 'germs' usually mean to people?
2 Describe how to make yoghurt.
3 Explain how making blue Stilton cheese is different from making ordinary cheese.
4 How could you make elderberry wine?

...bacteria   ...fungus (pl. fungi)   ...microbiologists

Microbiologists

One of the earliest **microbiologists** was Louis Pasteur. During his life (1822–1895), he solved various mysteries related to human health and contributed to the development of vaccination. It is largely because of him that microbiology exists as a separate area of science.

Microbiologists study microbes such as bacteria, viruses and fungi. Microbiologists are particularly interested in how microbes survive, how they affect us, and how we can use them.

Because microbes affect every aspect of our lives, microbiologists work in many different work environments. They are concerned with observing, identifying and monitoring microbes, developing new products (new ways of using the things that microbes produce) and identifying contamination.

Areas in which microbiologists work include:

- basic research
- medicine and healthcare
- the food industry
- industries such as pharmaceuticals, toiletries and biotechnology
- farming
- the environment.

The work a microbiologist might do includes:

- monitoring and testing samples
- developing computer software to work with microbes
- preventing the spread of disease and eliminating infections
- developing and evaluating products such as enzymes, vitamins, hormones and antibiotics
- producing new medicines
- growing specific microbe cultures, e.g. those used in the food and drink industry or in agriculture.

Microbiologists may also work in offices. Their work includes: keeping accurate records; writing up results from experiments; keeping up to date with new discoveries; and talking to non-scientists.

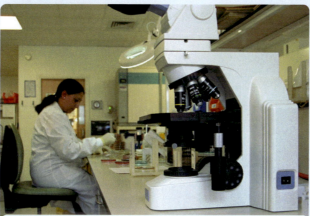

FIGURE 5: How might this modern microbiology laboratory differ from one Pasteur would have worked in?

QUESTIONS

5 What do microbiologists study?

6 State **three** ways in which the work of microbiologists affects your life.

7 Suggest why Louis Pasteur would find it hard to recognise the microbiology lab in figure 5.

Long life in yoghurt!

Farmer's wife and yoghurt producer Carol Duncan is set to discover the secret of long life ... in yoghurt. She is travelling to Russia – where people often live to 120 years of age – to discover the magic of their staple diet, a slightly alcoholic yoghurt made with yeast called kefir. Mrs Duncan already runs a yoghurt business with her husband in north Devon, using the herd of 100 cows on their family farm. She has now won a research scholarship to study the making of kefir and hopes it will become a British bestseller.

She said: "If you like yoghurt, you should love kefir, and there's no doubt it's very good for you. It contains a germ called *acidophilus*, which microbiologists have shown helps digestion – which may explain why these Russians live so long."

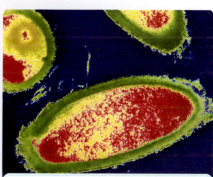

FIGURE 6: This is what makes yoghurt into kefir: *lactobacillus acidophilus*.

QUESTIONS

8 What does 'staple diet' mean?

9 What more scientific word could Carol have used instead of 'germ'?

10 As a microbiologist, you have been asked to design an experiment to investigate the effect of *Lactobacillus acidophilus* on digestion. Give as much detail as you can.

...microorganisms ...yeast

Pale and crunchy

INVESTIGATION

In some sorts of cooking, for example Chinese dishes, bean sprouts are a necessary ingredient. Food suppliers need to be able to see where there might be a demand for an ingredient, and also to know the key characteristics. Bean sprouts are best if they are pale in colour, with a crunchy texture.

The class that Sam is in has been set the task of investigating the conditions necessary to grow bean sprouts that are pale and crunchy.

He writes: "This is going to be important for the growers to know about. If they are to supply shops with produce to sell, they have to know what conditions to use to get the best results."

> 1A.1 Sam states a simple vocational application of his investigation and has clearly linked it in to a particular foodstuff. He could improve his mark by doing some more research and using this to explain why his investigation is important.

Sam's group decides that one key factor is the amount of light that the bean sprouts have, and another is the amount of water. They will set up their experiment so that they can carefully control each of these variables. They will then see which combination of factors produces bean sprouts with the best characteristics.

Sam's plan is shown below:
In our experiment we are going to plant seeds to grow bean sprouts. We think that the best way to grow pale, crunchy bean sprouts is to restrict the amount of light and also to restrict the amount of water. We think that plants grow pale if there isn't much light about, and also that too much water makes them limp. On the other hand, no light and no water wouldn't work.

What we are going to do in our experiment is to set up several trays of seedlings. Each tray will be kept under different conditions. We will compare the bean sprouts with examples from the supermarket to see which is closest.

We will restrict the light by putting a thin card cover over the tray of seedlings and cutting a window in the cover. We can alter the amount of light by altering the size of the window. We will grow the seedlings in a growing medium that is a bit like soil, but is made up of nutrients to encourage growth and has a loose structure so that it doesn't get waterlogged very easily.

Because the seedlings will be grown in laboratory conditions using scientific equipment, it won't be safe to taste them, but we can squeeze them to see if they feel the same and look at them to see if the colour is the same.

We are going to set up seven trays of seedlings. One (Tray Zero) is the control; we will have that out in the daylight and water it every day. The other six will be set up as shown in the table below.

Tray One Restricted light Growing medium watered every 6 hours	Tray Two Very restricted light Growing medium watered every 6 hours
Tray Three Restricted light Growing medium watered every 12 hours	Tray Four Very restricted light Growing medium watered every 12 hours
Tray Five Restricted light Growing medium watered every 24 hours	Tray Six Very restricted light Growing medium watered every 24 hours

2B.1 Sam has produced a plan for the investigation which is detailed enough to be followed by another person. To improve his mark, Sam could produce a more detailed plan for the investigation. How does he decide how much light to allow in?

STUDENT'S COMMENTARY

For the laboratory part, we completed a risk assessment form given to us by our teacher.

Risk Assessment form

DESCRIBE THE INVESTIGATION

We are going to grow bean shoots from seeds in different conditions. Some of the seeds will not have as much light and some will not have as much water.

WHAT ARE THE HAZARDS?

It isn't really a very dangerous experiment, but the water might get spilt or equipment might get knocked over. The seeds that are being grown with less light will have a cover over the top of the tray, and that might make it more likely that it would be knocked over. If the water got spilt, someone might slip.

WHAT ARE THE RISKS?

If someone slipped on a wet patch, they might be carrying something and it might hurt them.

HOW CAN THE RISK BE CONTROLLED?

The risk can be controlled by making sure that the trays are kept somewhere where they are not likely to get knocked. They will be kept low down so that it's less likely that they can drop. Any spillages of water will be cleared up straight away.

WHAT IS THE REMAINING RISK?

There then won't be much of a risk. I don't think this will be a dangerous experiment.

2B.2 Sam has carried out a risk assessment, but the form he used had very clear guidelines. He could improve his mark by carrying out the risk assessment more independently.

The results (after 7 days)

Tray	Bean sprouts
0	Too green, quite healthy but not very big.
1	Quite pale, healthy but not very big.
2	Pale, healthy but not very big.
3	Quite pale, rather small and spindly.
4	Pale, rather small and spindly.
5	Quite pale, rather weak.
6	Pale, very weak.

2C.1 Sam has selected the appropriate equipment for the investigation with a little guidance from his teacher and he has used it correctly and safely to carry out the plan to collect and record data accurately. To improve his work, Sam could also plan to repeat his measurements, as he is relying upon one set of results.

What the results showed

Two parts of our experiment went very well and as we expected. The results showed that we need to restrict the available light in order to make the bean sprouts pale. The control showed that the bean sprouts are too green for the retailers if the light is not restricted. The experiment also showed that the growing medium needs to be kept moist.
However, none of the seedlings looked like the ones from the supermarket. Some of them, especially in Trays One and Two, were the right colour, but not as plump in the stems.

2D.1 Sam has used the information collected from his investigations to draw some conclusions, which he has clearly based on careful observations. He could analyse his results in more detail and try to use more scientific ideas in suggesting what might have gone wrong.

My evaluation

I think we were on the right lines with this experiment in that we showed that restricting the amount of light keeps the bean sprouts pale and also tends to make them grow rather taller. However, our shoots didn't grow anywhere near as big as the shop ones. This could be because:

- we hadn't left them long enough
- the growing medium wasn't right
- some other condition, (such as the temperature) was wrong.

If we did the experiment again, I would certainly try leaving the shoots for longer. I would also do some research into growing mediums. A garden centre might be able to tell me what I could use to grow the seedlings in.

The kind of information that tests like this produce would be very useful indeed to someone growing bean sprouts to supply shops. It would tell them the conditions to use to get the right colour and size. The grower needs to know what equipment to have available and when to start growing the shoots so that they are ready for the retailer.

2E.1 Sam has evaluated his investigation and made valid suggestions as to how to improve it. He has thought carefully about what it showed and could work on this more to indicate how the improvements would give better quality data.

2E.2 Sam has suggested how the findings from his investigation could be used in the context of the food supply industry, but he needs to develop his ideas rather more to get a better mark.

Food poisoning

You will find out:
- What food poisoning is and what causes it
- How to prevent food poisoning
- How the risk of food poisoning can be controlled

Washing your hands – does it make a difference?

Although many microorganisms are safe, there are some that can make you ill. Every year people die from food poisoning. Microbes are found everywhere – in the air you breathe, as well as on your body. Even after washing your hands, microbes are there on your skin.

FIGURE 1: Are your hands clean? This handprint shows how many bacteria there might be on your hands.

What bacteria like

Although **bacteria** are **microorganisms**, they are a bit like us! To survive, they like it warm – about 37 °C; they like food – for energy and to grow; and they also like it moist (this is not like us, although we still need water to survive).

Bacteria that cause food poisoning

There are many different bacteria that can cause **food poisoning**. As they grow, they produce **toxins** (poisons) and it is these that make you ill. Here are three of the most common bacteria:

Bacterium	Where it is found	Risky foods	Time for illness to develop	Symptoms
Campylobacter	raw meat and poultry	• undercooked chicken • raw milk • cross-contaminated food	3–5 days from eating infected food	• fever • stomach pains • diarrhoea
E. coli (full name *Escherichia coli*)	in the guts of all humans and many animals	• undercooked meat • milk • cross-contaminated food	3–4 days	• vomiting • diarrhoea
Salmonella	in the gut of animals and birds, spread by faeces (solid waste) in water and on food	• chicken • raw eggs • food containing raw eggs • vegetables	6–48 hours	• headaches • diarrhoea • vomiting

TABLE 1: Common disease-causing bacteria.

QUESTIONS

1. What conditions do bacteria need to survive?
2. What are toxins?
3. Which food poisoning develops the quickest?
4. Which symptom is common to all three types of food poisoning?
5. What **one** thing should you do to food to prevent food poisoning?

Stopping bacteria from spreading

Food preparation areas, like food counters in shops and kitchens, have to be kept free from bacteria. This can be done by:

- using disinfectants and detergents
- high standards of personal **hygiene**
- controlling (killing) pests like mice and insects.
- sterilising utensils
- disposing of waste properly

Stopping bacteria from growing

Bacteria like it warm and damp, with a supply of food. If you change one of these conditions, bacteria stop growing and die.

Conditions	What happens	Useful for
Too hot for comfort	High temperatures kill many bacteria so after heating, so the food is put into sterile containers.	
Chilled out	Most bacteria stop growing at about 5 °C; fridges are slightly colder and freezers are at −20 °C.	
Too salty	Bacteria dehydrate when they are put into a strong salt solution.	
Too dry	Bacteria need water to grow and stay alive.	
Acid bath	Pickling food in vinegar prevents most bacteria from growing well.	

TABLE 2: Preserving food – stopping bacteria from growing.

Checking up on bacteria

Controlling where bacteria grow is very important. If they are found near food then there is a high risk of diseases spreading. **Public Health Inspectors** are responsible for checking that bacteria don't grow where they shouldn't.

Sometimes bacteria contaminate food, and this can lead to food products being withdrawn from the shops. This in turn can result in health scares.

QUESTIONS

6 Suggest **three** things that can be done to keep areas where food is prepared free from bacteria.

7 What effect does a high temperature have on bacteria?

8 Why does keeping food dry stop bacteria from growing?

9 What do Public Health Inspectors do?

Pickling food in vinegar prevents most bacteria from growing

Cadbury withdraw a million chocolate bars

In the summer of 2006, Cadbury had a health scare. They recalled over a million bars of chocolate from shops after minute levels of *Salmonella* were found. Their spokesperson said that: "The recall is precautionary and the risk is low. Cadbury have been manufacturing chocolate for more than 100 years and have always treated public wellbeing as its highest priority." He went on to say that Cadbury were "absolutely satisfied" that their products were safe to eat. The levels of contamination were "significantly below the standard that would be any health problem".

However, bacteriologist and microbiologist Professor Hugh Pennington, of Aberdeen University, said that the only safe level of *Salmonella* in chocolate was "zero".

FIGURE 2: Do you remember the Cadbury health scare?

QUESTIONS

10 Why did Cadbury recall so many chocolate bars?

11 In your group, draw up lists of pros and cons for companies who recall products like Cadbury did. Discuss whether such recalls of products from shops lead to public scares or add to public confidence in food manufacturing companies.

...*microorganisms* ...*Public Health Inspectors* ...*toxins*

Practical microbiology

You will find out:
- How to carry out basic food microbiological techniques
- Why it is important to be aseptic
- How to count bacteria
- How to identify bacteria

Agar plates for growing bacteria

Like us, bacteria need food and water to grow. They also need an optimum temperature. The bacteria growing on these **agar plates** in figure 1 were put there by a microbiologist. A special technique was used to prevent contamination. The agar jelly contains nutrients and the Petri dishes were kept at the right temperature.

FIGURE 1: Petri dishes containing bacterial cultures.

Aseptic technique

Aseptic means 'no microbes'. Microbiologists must investigate microbes without any **contamination**. They must:

- wash hands and laboratory benches with disinfectant
- sterilise apparatus in a special pressure cooker, called an autoclave.

FIGURE 2: An industrial-sized autoclave; at school you can use a domestic pressure cooker.

How to make sterile agar plates

Agar tablets containing nutrients are mixed with water and sterilised. The mixture is then poured into sterile Petri dishes. The agar plates are used to grow bacteria and other microbes. Microbiologists do this when investigating, for example, food poisoning. They take samples of the suspect food and samples from where it was prepared.

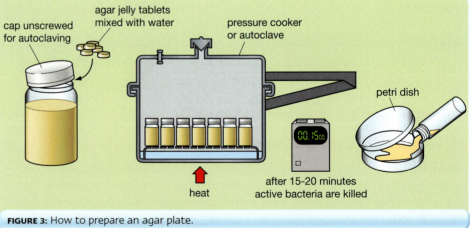

cap unscrewed for autoclaving

agar jelly tablets mixed with water

pressure cooker or autoclave

petri dish

heat

after 15-20 minutes active bacteria are killed

FIGURE 3: How to prepare an agar plate.

Streak plates

Making a **streak plate** allows you to produce single colonies of bacteria that are all the same type (the same species). This is what you do:

1 Heat up your inoculating loop until it is red-hot (this will sterilise it) and let it cool.

2 Use it to remove a small amount of what is to be tested.

3 Streak the loop on the agar plate. This will produce an area with lots of bacteria (see **a** in figure 4).

4 Flame your loop again and let it cool.

Like us, bacteria need food and water to grow.

...agar plates ...aseptic ...contamination

5 Go back to the edge of the first area on your agar plate and extend the streaks. This will produce an area with less bacteria (see **b** in figure 4).

Then continue to extend the streaks to produce areas **c**, **d** and **e**, remembering to flame the loop (to kill any bacteria that are left on it) before using it each time.

Seal the dish with two small bits of tape so that the lid cannot come off accidentally. Incubate the plate for 48 hours. Different species of bacteria will show up as separate colonies (blobs) on the agar plate. They may be different colours.

Serial dilution

Sometimes the sample you are investigating is so full of bacteria that it is impossible to count them. A **serial dilution** lets you dilute your sample by a known amount. You can then grow a diluted sample, count how many colonies you have and multiply it up by the amount you diluted it down.

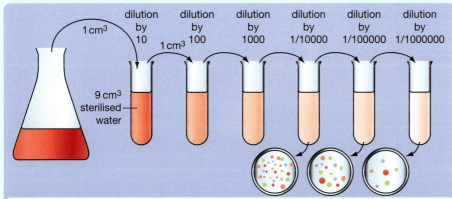

FIGURE 5: Serial dilution will make it easier to count the number of bacterial colonies.

Compare the numbers of bacteria in fresh milk and stale milk

Fresh milk goes 'off' quickly if left out of the fridge – this is caused by bacteria. A microbiologist set up the following experiment:

- 1 cm³ of fresh milk was placed onto an agar plate and evenly spread out with a glass rod.
- 1 cm³ of stale milk (left out of a fridge for 24 hours) was put onto another agar plate.

FIGURE 6: Which plate has stale milk on it? How can you tell?

Both agar plates were placed in an incubator for 2 days. Figure 6 shows the plates.

QUESTIONS

1 What does 'aseptic' mean?
2 Write a paragraph to describe how you prepare an agar plate.
3 Explain what a 'streak plate' is.
4 When would a microbiologist want to use a 'serial dilution'?

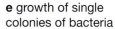
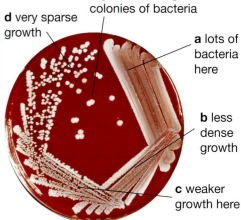

d very sparse growth

e growth of single colonies of bacteria

a lots of bacteria here

b less dense growth

c weaker growth here

FIGURE 4: How to streak an agar plate.

Bacterial growth

Bacteria were grown in a nutrient broth (a bit like agar jelly, only a liquid). The numbers of bacteria recorded over a 2-day period were:

Time/h	Number of bacteria in millions	
	Living	Living and dead
0	9	10
1	10	11
2	11	12
5	18	21
10	390	440
12	540	610
15	540	690
24	540	750
30	540	960
36	230	960
45	30	960

TABLE 1: Growth of bacteria over two days.

QUESTIONS

5 Draw a graph of the number of living bacteria against time.
6 Draw another graph to show the number of dead bacteria.
7 Suggest **one** reason why the number of living bacteria falls.
8 What could be done to stop the number falling so steeply?

Types of farming

You will find out:
- That there are two different approaches to farming – organic and intensive
- What the advantages and disadvantages are of these two methods of farming

Farming and the landscape

Farming has made the landscape. Farmers decide which crops to grow or animals to have on their farms. Farms often specialise in cultivating one product. Hedgerows have been removed and fields are enormous. On many farms, the use of chemicals is widespread. But some farmers believe that employing artificial means for production is wrong. So what's best?

Farming methods

There are two main types of farm:
- **intensive** farms ■ **organic** farms.

There are advantages and disadvantages to both types.

Intensive farms

These produce large amounts of food cheaply and efficiently, by maximising the growth of crops and livestock.

Advantages	Disadvantages
Livestock	
Animals can be kept in 'optimum' conditions for growth.	Animals could suffer from stress from overcrowding. Pollution from animal waste.
Hormones and high-protein feeds used to promote meat production.	Hormones enter the human food chain (consequences not fully understood).
Animal health is maintained by antibiotics and other drugs.	Animals can become resistant to antibiotics.
Crops	
Chemical fertilisers are used to increase growth.	These damage habitats when washed into streams, rivers and ponds.
Chemical pesticides are used to kill pest species.	These kill beneficial species too.
Machinery means fewer people are employed.	Uses non-renewable energy – petrol/diesel/oil.
Enormous fields of a single crop (called monoculture).	This can lead to reduction of soil nutrients.

TABLE 1: Advantages and disadvantages of intensive farming.

Organic farms

Organic farmers use organic principles when they produce food:
- They respect their animals.
- They only use **natural fertilisers** – manure.
- They remove weeds rather than killing them with pesticides.
- They encourage natural pest control methods, e.g. encouraging ladybirds to eat greenfly.
- They try to be as sustainable as possible.

Some people believe these principles are good and are prepared to pay more for food produced in a more environmentally friendly way.

QUESTIONS

1 Why do we need farmers?
2 What are the **two** main ways of farming?
3 List **three** differences between these two methods of farming.
4 Why are some people prepared to pay more for organic food?

Crops, chemicals and keeping the soil fertile

Plants need various essential **nutrients** for healthy growth (see table 2).

As crops grow, their roots absorb nutrients from the soil. Intensive farming methods involve replacing these nutrients by adding artificial fertilisers to the soil. This means that the same crop can be grown again and again in subsequent years. Organic farmers use crop rotation and set-aside land to keep soil fertile.

Name of nutrient	Effect on plant if absent
nitrates	yellow leaves and a weak stem
phosphates	poor root growth
potassium	flowers do not develop properly
magnesium	leaves turn yellow

TABLE 2: Nutrients needed by plants.

FIGURE 1: A farmer spraying his crops with herbicides – what could he do instead of using these chemicals?

Animal welfare

Intensive farmers keep livestock (e.g. pigs and hens) in buildings. This means that their surroundings can be closely controlled:

- Food: provided to optimise weight gain (produce more meat).
- Space: movement is restricted so that animals do not waste energy moving about.
- Temperature: animals are kept warm so that they do not squander energy maintaining their body temperature.

As a result of this, livestock convert more of the energy in the food they eat into meat because they do not use it to move about or keep warm.

Organic farmers try to keep their livestock under more natural conditions, out in open fields. This means that the animals are free to move about.

FIGURE 2: Cooped up in a battery or kept outside in the fresh air. Which would you prefer?

FIGURE 3: Do you think these pigs are 'happy' being kept in free-range conditions?

QUESTIONS

5 Why do plants need essential nutrients?

6 Explain why intensive farmers use chemical fertilisers.

7 What do organic farmers do instead of using chemical fertilisers?

8 Why do intensive farmers keep their livestock under controlled conditions?

Fertilisers and river pollution

This river, in East Anglia, is choked by water weeds. It flows through a nature reserve. A local farmer used too much fertiliser on his land and this was washed into the river by a heavy downpour of rain. The fertiliser caused rapid growth of the water plants. The water became clogged with vegetation and this blocked out the light. The water plants died, and as they were decomposed by water-dwelling bacteria all the oxygen was used up. This means that almost nothing else is able to live in the river – just some anaerobic bacteria, which create a 'bad eggs' smell.

FIGURE 4: Pollution caused by fertiliser.

QUESTIONS

9 Farmers using intensive methods of food production use fertilisers. What could this farmer have done to prevent the pollution his actions have caused?

10 What could the local council, or the government, do to prevent the farmer from polluting the river?

11 The charity that is in charge of the nature reserve is worried that its colony of very rare waterfowl (birds) will die because their habitat has been damaged. Suggest what they could do to ensure their survival.

...nutrients ...organic

Growing plants

You will find out:
- How to plan a plant growth experiment
- How to assess the results from such experiments

Germinating seeds

When seeds are given the correct conditions, they germinate. This means they start to grow. First a tiny root pokes out of the seed coat. Then a shoot starts to grow. Eventually green leaves can be seen. But what are the optimum conditions for plant growth?

FIGURE 1: What conditions does this seed need to germinate?

What plants need to grow

Plants need the following things to **grow**:

- Oxygen from the air – the seeds need to respire to release energy needed to grow and germinate.
- Light – for photosynthesis.
- Water from the soil and carbon dioxide from the air – for photosynthesis.
- Minerals – from the soil.

Plants use water and carbon dioxide to make sugar. They then convert these sugars into starch, fats and oils, all of which are needed for growth. However, to make proteins, plants also need other chemicals – minerals. Farmers add these minerals to their land as fertilisers. You can learn more about fertilisers on pages 58–59.

Here are three **investigations** you can try:

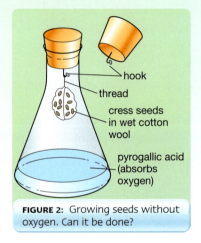

FIGURE 2: Growing seeds without oxygen. Can it be done?

Oxygen

Figure 2 shows you how to set up this experiment. What other flask will you have to set up as a comparison (a control)?

Light

Sprinkle some cress seeds onto wet cotton wool in two clean Petri dish lids or bases. Put one in the dark and keep the other in the light. Make sure you water them regularly. What do they look like after 5–6 days?

Water

Plants are constantly losing water through their leaves. If it is lost faster than it is absorbed by the roots, the plant will not grow – it will wilt and eventually die.

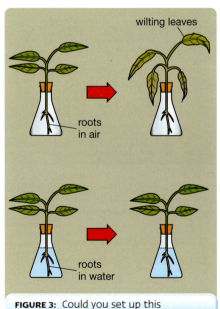

FIGURE 3: Could you set up this experiment? How can you tell which plant is healthy?

QUESTIONS

1   Why do seeds need oxygen?
2   Why is photosynthesis important if a plant is to grow?
3   What do plants look like that have been grown in the dark?
4   What happens to a plant when it wilts?

...experiment   ...grow

Minerals

At home you can add 'plant food' to your pot plants to make them grow better, but how much should you use?

Catrina, a plant biologist, wanted to find out what was the best concentration of plant food to use. She used cress seeds for her **experiment**. She watered them every day. A week after they started to grow, she measured the lengths of ten stems from each batch. Here are her results:

FIGURE 4: Plant foods – fertiliser for potted plants.

Drops of liquid plant food dissolved in 500 cm³ of distilled water	Mean length of cress stems/mm
0	20
2	24
4	31
6	35
8	39
10	44

TABLE 1: Plant food growth experiment results.

Here is a list of the apparatus she used:

- Petri dish lids/bases, or other small dishes
- blotting paper
- cress seeds
- plant food
- 10 cm³ measuring cylinder/pipette
- 500 cm³ beakers
- ruler.

FIGURE 5: Catrina measuring seedlings.

QUESTIONS

5 What do 'plant foods' contain?

6 Draw a line graph of Catrina's results.

7 What further experiments could Catrina do?

8 Read through the apparatus that Catrina used. Write a paragraph to explain how she would have used each thing in the list.

Minerals and plant growth

General-purpose agricultural fertilisers contain the following elements:

- nitrogen
- phosphorus
- potassium.

Plants need these to grow and develop properly. When deficiency symptoms appear in crops, the soil can be analysed. This will confirm the exact mineral deficiency. The plants in figure 6 show some of the symptoms of mineral deficiencies. Farmers have to decide how much fertilizer to add to their land.

nitrogen

upper leaves light green, lower leaves yellow

nitrogen is found in proteins

phosphorus

stunted growth, leaves abnormally dark, often developing a red/purple colour

phosphorus is found in DNA

potassium

yellowing at tips and margins of older leaves; dead spots on leaves

potassium helps enzymes to work properly

FIGURE 6: Plants showing mineral deficiencies.

QUESTIONS

9 What do plants use nitrogen for?

10 How would you know whether a plant lacked phosphorus?

11 Design an experiment that would help the farmer decide how much fertiliser to use.

...investigations

Frozen fresh

INVESTIGATION

In this investigation, a group of students investigated the use of freezing as a way of storing food. Freezing has been used since 1930 as a means of preserving food, but there are some foodstuffs that freezing is less effective on.

Rosie's group had set up a series of experiments to find out about freezing and which foods it works well on. She wrote:

"We started our investigation by going to a local supermarket and looking to see which foods were available in frozen form and which weren't. We wanted to find out why certain foods can't be frozen and to see what happens if they are. This kind of information would be very useful to people working in the food processing and retail trades. Frozen foods are an effective way of keeping food for long periods of time, until it is needed. We decided to concentrate on fruit and vegetables. Texture is important with both of these and we thought that it might be that freezing some foods might spoil the texture. Freshness is also important, and some fruit and vegetables go off quickly, so preserving them is important.

People running supermarkets and other food shops could be very interested in this information."

> 2A.1 Rosie states a vocational application of her investigation and explains why she has decided to investigate this particular area. She could improve her mark by doing some more detailed research and using this to explain why her investigation is important.

Here is Rosie's report:

When we went round the supermarket, we found foods that you can buy frozen include:

- chips
- broccoli
- sweet corn
- carrots
- peas

Foods that you can't buy frozen include:

- strawberries (although we did find frozen cheesecake with strawberry topping)
- raspberries
- apples (although we did find frozen apple pie)
- potatoes (although we did find frozen chips)
- onions (though we did find frozen onion rings).

We noticed there were some fruits that you couldn't buy frozen but that you could buy tinned, such as peaches and oranges. We then came up with two ideas:

- Foods that have quite a long shelf life, such as potatoes, onions and apples, aren't frozen because there isn't such a great need and it takes more energy to freeze food (and to keep it frozen) than not.
- Soft fruits such as strawberries and raspberries might be damaged by the freezing process. This might not matter so much if they are in the form of a topping or filling.

The next part of our investigation was to get some fresh strawberries and some fresh raspberries and to put them in freezer bags (separately) in a freezer. After 48 hours, we took them out, allowed them to thaw and examined them.

1B.1 Rosie has produced a simple plan for the investigation, which makes it quite clear what has been done and why. It could be developed to include a more comprehensive range of fruit and vegetables and more research into other methods of preserving fruit and vegetables, such as drying or chilling.

Frozen fresh

STUDENT'S COMMENTARY

There wasn't much about this investigation that would be dangerous, but we filled in a risk assessment form just to make sure.

Risk Assessment Form

DESCRIBE THE INVESTIGATION

We are going to find out what happens when strawberries and raspberries are frozen and then thawed. We are going to put them in freezer bags and then into the freezer and get them out the next lesson. We will then put samples under a microscope to look at them closely.

WHAT ARE THE HAZARDS?

There isn't much of a hazard with putting food in a freezer, but there is when you take it out because it is so cold. There is a hazard with using microscopes because they are heavy and might drop on your foot, and the slides and cover slips are made of glass.

WHAT ARE THE RISKS?

Your hands will get cold from handling the frozen food. If they get numb, you might be more likely to drop a microscope on your foot or you might cut yourself on the glass from the microscope.

HOW CAN THE RISK BE CONTROLLED?

We will wear gloves when taking food out of the freezer. We will be careful with the microscopes. We will be careful with the microscope slides and cover slips, not leaving them on the bench tops.

WHAT IS THE REMAINING RISK?

I think that we can work safely if we do the things that I said.

1B.2 Rosie has completed a risk assessment using a detailed form. More independent work on her part in this area might have produced a higher mark.

What we found out

Both the strawberries and the raspberries were disgusting when they were thawed. They were like pulp and didn't look attractive. The taste was quite different. You could tell what fruit they were but the texture was different and nowhere near as nice. You couldn't put them on display in a shop and expect people to buy them.

This would explain why the strawberry cheesecake could be frozen. The topping was a kind of fruit puree in which it didn't matter that the individual strawberries had lost much of their shape.

We then tried to find out what had happened to the fruit when it was frozen. We made slides of the strawberry and raspberry to put under a microscope. It wasn't possible to see individual cells; the tissues just seemed to be a mess. We then did some research on the Internet and found out several things:

- The cell membranes in soft fruit are easily damaged. When water freezes it forms crystals and these are larger than the water so they may damage the cells. This becomes apparent when the frozen fruit thaws.

- You can get frozen raspberries. They are frozen very quickly as soon as they are picked. This reduces the damage to cells. The equipment used freezes food much quicker than a domestic freezer can.

Then we interviewed some adults about frozen foods. We asked them if they found it a nuisance not being able to buy frozen strawberries.

- Four people we asked said they didn't mind.
- Two people said it was a nuisance.
- Three people said that it was a pity but that preserved food didn't taste as nice as fresh.
- One person said she only ate food that was healthy. If you froze it, it wouldn't be healthy.

> 2C.1 Rosie has used appropriate equipment and gathered a lot of relevant information. The data was presented in a clear and appropriate way. The research on the Internet was relevant but could have included more detail about such aspects as the effect of freezing on cell structure. The views of people were well presented but the sample group could have been larger to make it more representative.

What we learned

We learned several things from this investigation:

- Freezing vegetables seems to work much better than freezing fruit.
- Some fruit you can't freeze (at least, not very easily) but you can tin them.
- Soft fruits are particularly difficult to freeze without losing texture, particularly at home.
- If the fruit is in a puree, it is much easier to freeze without spoiling it.

- Some people wouldn't buy frozen fruit even if it was available because they think it spoils the flavour and makes it less healthy.

> 2D.1 Rosie has gathered together various pieces of evidence in order to produce several conclusions. The conclusions are very relevant to the investigation but are based on rather limited information.

My evaluation

The investigation was a success because we found out a lot about frozen foods, especially strawberries. We could have developed it more by looking at other kinds of fruit. It would be good to come up with a better way to preserve strawberries, but that seems quite difficult.

I think our work might be of interest to shop managers but it wouldn't tell them how to preserve fruit.

> 1E.1 Rosie has given a simple evaluation of the investigation and suggested an improvement but hasn't given enough detail, bearing in mind the range of conclusions she had drawn and the scope of the investigation.

Ideas for investigations

Julie is in bed, having fainted earlier in the day because of iron deficiency, or anaemia. Her partner Paul has gone to the shops to get some iron tablets. He went into the chemist and was directed to a display. There were lots of iron tablets – but which to buy? Surely iron is iron – could one be better than another? Paul chose one brand, mainly because it seemed to be selling better, but might there be a difference? How could iron tablets be tested for the amount of iron they contain?

Fazila and Rosie are walking back from school and call in at the local shop to get drinks. They both want to get fruit juice, but there's a huge choice. How could you compare fruit juices by testing them? What types of nutrients could you test the drinks for? What other tests or examinations could you carry out? How could you test for suspended matter? Do you think the results would vary much from one juice to another?

Paul grows all his own vegetables, but is sometimes disappointed that they don't grow very big. He sees various types of 'plant food' in his garden centre and wonders if they are any good. How could he test the 'plant foods' to compare them and to see if they'll help him to grow bigger vegetables?

Emma seems to have one cold after another. Her father tells her she should take more Vitamin C and that fruit juice is a good way of doing it. She doesn't really like fruit juice, but doesn't like the colds either. She thinks that if she could find out which type of fruit juice had the most Vitamin C in it, she wouldn't have to drink as much. How could she test a number of different juices to compare the amount of Vitamin C in each?

Abi has decided to base an investigation on the conditions necessary for bacteria to grow. She has heard that toothpaste inhibits the growth of bacteria and is interested to see whether the make of toothpaste makes any difference. How could she set up her investigation to see if this is the case?

What should I include?

To complete your investigation you need to:
- explain how your investigation can help to analyse the food, drug or substance
- produce a plan that is detailed enough for someone else to be able to follow
- carry out a risk assessment
- decide what equipment to use in your investigation
- carry out your plan carefully and collect and record your results
- process your results and explain your conclusions
- evaluate your investigation, explaining its strengths and weaknesses
- explain how your findings can be used to assist with the testing of that substance.

Unit summary

Concept map

Food

Food consists of carbohydrates, proteins, fats, vitamins, minerals, water and dietary fibre.

Food additives improve taste and appearance as well as increasing shelf life.

Food is needed for energy, growth, repair and keeping healthy.

Vitamins, minerals and fibre are needed for health.

Your required diet depends on who you are and what you do.

Food tests

Food tests can be carried out on food to see what it contains.

DCPIP is a test for vitamin C.

Starch, fat, protein and reducing sugar (glucose) are easy to test for.

Microbiology

Microbes are found almost everywhere.

Microbes can be grown using sterile agar plates and aseptic techniques.

Microbes can be used to make food, including yoghurt, cheese, beer, wine and bread

Some microbes cause food poisoning by producing toxins.

Farming

Intensive farms use lots of fertilisers and pesticides to increase the production of crops and livestock.

Plants need oxygen, light, water, carbon dioxide and various minerals to grow properly.

Organic farms use natural fertilisers and remove pests mechanically, rather than with artificial chemicals.

Unit quiz

1 Give **four** reasons why we need food.

2 Why do you need carbohydrates?

3 What happens if your diet lacks vitamin D?

4 Which mineral do you need to avoid being anaemic?

5 Why is dietary fibre important in your diet?

6 Why are food additives used?

7 Describe a food test for glucose.

8 What are microorganisms?

9 Why do some bacteria cause food poisoning?

10 What would a microbiologist use a streak plate for?

11 What are the two main ways of running farms?

12 How do plants get the minerals they need?

Literacy activity

Microbes

Microbes were first described by a famous Dutch scientist, Antoni van Leeuwenhoek, in the 17th century, in a fascinating sequence of letters to the Royal Society of London. He had constructed for himself a primitive but very effective microscope (shown on the right) and in his letters described the extraordinary menagerie of 'animalcules' he had observed in samples of canal water, broth, vinegar, saliva and so on. Leeuwenhoek's drawings leave no doubt that, among tiny worms, water fleas, particulate matter, etc., he saw normally invisible creatures: the bacteria, yeasts and protozoa that we now call microbes.

QUESTIONS

1 In sentence 2, what does the word 'effective' mean?

2 Suggest another phrase for 'extraordinary menagerie', also in sentence 2.

3 Why were bacteria, yeasts and protozoa 'normally invisible'?

1 A dietician produced this table of data about some foods:

Food	kJ/25 g	Carbohydrate (g)	Protein (g)	Fat (g)	Calcium (mg)	Vitamin C (mg)	Vitamin D (mg)
White bread	290	14.8	2.3	0.5	25	0	0
Butter	950	0	0.2	24.2	5	0	11
Cheese	500	0	7.3	9.9	240	0	4
Potatoes	100	6.1	0.5	0	2	2.5	0
Blackcurrants	35	1.8	0.4	0	18	58	0

a Which food is the highest in protein? [1]
b Which food has the lowest energy content? [1]
c Which food is best for healthy bone formation? [1]
d Which food would you recommend to prevent scurvy? [1]
e How much energy would you obtain if you ate a sandwich containing 125 g of bread, 50 g of cheese and 5 g of butter? [2]

 2 Here is a label showing the nutritional information from a carton of ready-made custard.

Maud's own 'Home-made' custard
(just like Granny used to make!)

Nutritional information

Nutrient	Content/100g
Energy	425kJ
Carbohydrates	15.8g
Proteins	4.6g
Fats	3.2g
Fibre	0.1g
Sodium	0.04g

Shake carton well before opening. Refrigerate after opening. Consume within three days of opening. Contains no artificial preservatives or colours.

1 kg

a What is the total mass of the nutrients in 100 g of Maud's own 'home-made' custard? [2]
b Why does your answer to **a** above not add up to 100? What is missing? [2]
c Calculate the total mass of carbohydrate in this container of custard. [2]
d Once opened, why does the custard have to be **(i)** stored in a fridge; and **(ii)** eaten within three days? [2]
e The label tells you that the custard contains no artificial preservatives or colours. What is a preservative? [1]

 3 Many microbiologists are involved in the food industry. Their work often involves the prevention of food poisoning.

a Which groups of organisms do microbiologists study? [1]
b Which group of microorganisms is usually involved in food poisoning? [1]
c Suggest **two** ways in which these microorganisms contaminate the food you eat. [2]
d List **three** ways in which food poisoning can be prevented. [3]
e Bacteria can reproduce by simply dividing in two. Given optimum conditions, they will divide every 30 minutes. Complete this table and draw a graph of the numbers. [5]

Time (min)	0	30	60	90	120	150	180	210
Number of bacteria	1	2	4	?	?	?	?	?

 4 Organic food is more expensive than food produced by intensive methods. In spite of the growing demand for organic food, its manufacture only accounts for a small proportion of Britain's total food production.

a Explain the main difference between intensive farming and organic farming. [1]
b Give one reason why you might buy food produced by intensive methods. [1]
c Give two reasons why you would buy organically produced food. [2]
d Explain why organically produced food is more expensive than food produced by intensive methods. [2]

(Total 33 marks)

Farmers often add fertilisers to their fields so that crops grow more. These fertilisers contain nitrogen, phosphorus and potassium.

a   Explain why each of these is needed:
   (i) nitrogen [1]
   (ii) phosphorus [1]
   (iii) potassium [1]
b   A plant biologist tested a new liquid fertiliser, called 'Speedy-Grow', to find the best concentration to use on tomato plants. She added different concentrations of 'Speedy-Grow' to tomato plants and then measured the diameter of the tomatoes that she got from the plants. Her results are in the table.
   (i)   Draw a line graph of these results. [4]
   (ii) What is the optimum concentration for 'Speedy-Grow'? Explain your answer. [3]

Concentration of 'Speedy-Grow'(g/litre of water)	0	5	10	15	20	25	30	35	40
Diameter of tomatoes (mm)	00	250	300	365	400	400	380	250	plants died

The student has given specific examples of why these nutrients are needed and therefore gains full marks. Be sure to avoid general statement like 'for healthy growth' or 'to be healthy'.

The student has given the correct answer but has not explained it, so only gets one mark. To get the full three marks, he/she would need to explain that the curve levels off at this point and that beyond 30 g/litre it starts to drop.

a   i   Nitrogen is needed for making enzymes and other proteins.
    ii Phosphorus is needed for making new cells; it's found in DNA.
    iii Potassium is needed to help make enzymes work properly.
b   i   This is a line graph showing the results.

A line graph, not a block graph or histogram or scattergram, is asked for, so there should be no line of best fit. The student has correctly joined each point. Marks are awarded as shown below, so the student gains full marks. 'Speedy-Grow' concentration on the x-axis; this is the independent variable [1] Size of tomatoes as diameter in mm on the y-axis; this is the dependent variable [1] Points plotted correctly and accurately [1] Line joining the points [1] Use a ruler to draw the x-axis and y-axis; scales have to be properly spaced.

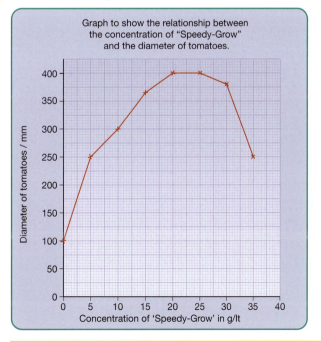

Graph to show the relationship between the concentration of "Speedy-Grow" and the diameter of tomatoes.

   ii The optimum concentration of 'Speedy-Grow' is 20 g per litre of water.

Overall grade: B

How to get an A

Read the question carefully; make sure you understand what you are being asked to do.

Make a different point for each mark, so if a question is worth three marks you will have to give three different bits of information to get full marks. Saying the same thing three times will not earn you three marks.

DISCOVER FACIAL RECONSTRUCTION!

Forensic scientists carry out facial reconstructions when they need to identify human remains. This provides a likeness of the victim which might allow them to be identified from records of missing persons, for example.

Modelling clay is placed over a plaster cast of the skull.

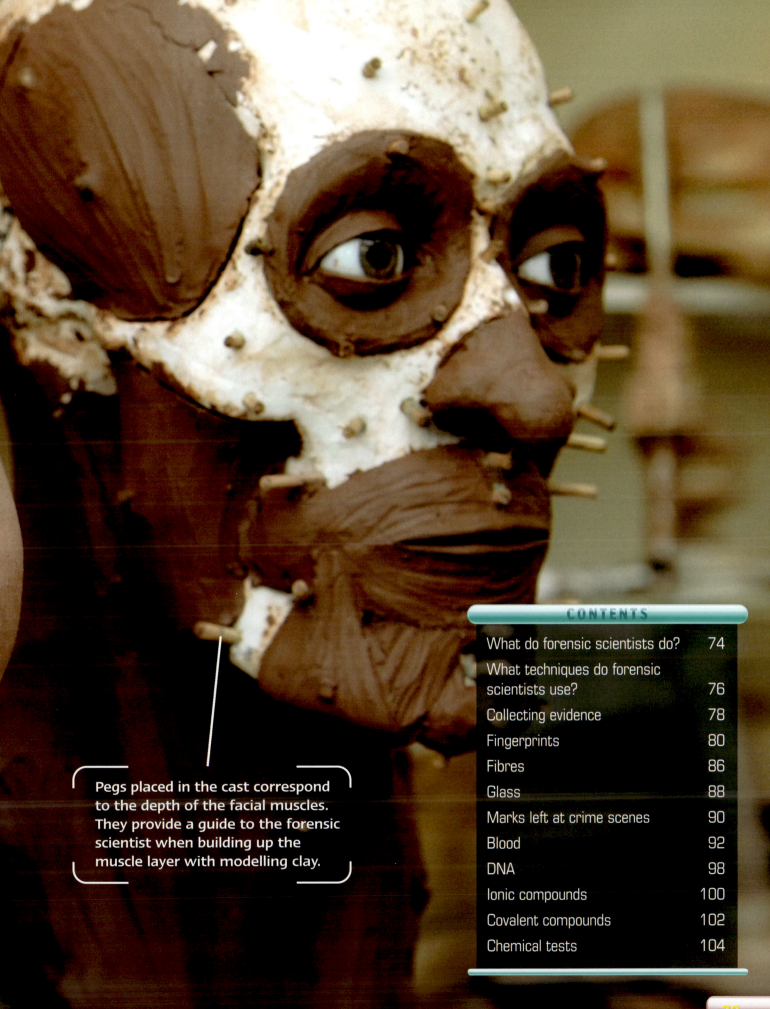

Pegs placed in the cast correspond to the depth of the facial muscles. They provide a guide to the forensic scientist when building up the muscle layer with modelling clay.

CONTENTS

What do forensic scientists do?

You will find out:

- How forensic scientists help the police to investigate crimes
- How forensic methods can be used in archaeology, to investigate industrial accidents and to find out whether people are related or not

London bombings

On 7 July 2005, suicide bombers exploded bombs on three tube trains and a bus in London. It was the bloodiest day that London had witnessed since the Second World War. The explosions killed 56 people, injured many more and caused enormous damage. Once the emergency services had rescued the injured and removed the dead, teams of forensic scientists took over the crime scene. They sorted through the scenes of carnage to piece together what had happened, to try and prevent similar events happening in the future.

FIGURE 1: Forensic scientists had to sort through the scenes of carnage after the bombs went off.

What is forensic science?

Forensic science is science that is used to help the law. In court cases forensic science can provide valuable **evidence** for the defence or the prosecution, but forensic scientists are **impartial** and **unbiased** – their aim is to find information to help them find out the truth about what has happened.

The Forensic Science Service is a government agency that provides scientific expertise to police forces in England and Wales. Evidence is removed from crime or accident scenes by specially trained Scene of Crime Officers (**SOCOs**) and sent to special laboratories for analysis. Forensic science evidence now plays an important part in the prosecution case of most serious crimes, such as murders and rapes.

There are many different **techniques** used in forensic science. The one chosen will depend on the evidence available and the information required.

Forensic science techniques have many applications. Sometimes forensic scientists study DNA evidence. **DNA** is found in the nucleus of a cell. As well as being a very powerful way of identifying victims, suspects or witnesses from crime scenes, it can also be used to:

- prove whether a child belongs to a parent
- resolve problems over inheritance
- provide information from archaeological evidence
- work out exactly why industrial accidents have happened.

Forensic science evidence now plays an important part in the prosecution case of most serious crimes

---

QUESTIONS

1 What is forensic science?

2 What is the Forensic Science Service?

3 What is a SOCO?

4 Why might a forensic scientist be sent to the scene of an industrial accident?

...DNA ...evidence ...forensic ...impartial

How are paternity tests carried out?

If there is doubt over the identity of a child's father, it can be solved by a paternity test. A doctor or nurse takes a sample from each of the parents and the child. The sample can either be taken by gently scraping a mouth swab against the inside of the cheek to remove some cells or by taking a small blood sample. The samples are then sent to a Paternity Testing Unit for comparison. This technique can also be used to resolve uncertainties about other family relationships, so it can be useful in many situations such as immigration cases.

FIGURE 2: Paternity tests can be used to prove family relationships.

Why do forensic scientists investigate industrial accidents?

Forensic scientists are routinely called to the scenes of industrial accidents, including fires and explosions. These scientists study the evidence at the scene, in order to understand the chain of events that led to the accident taking place. By understanding why an accident has happened, we can take steps to prevent a similar thing happening in the future.

Why do archaeologists use forensic techniques?

Archaeologists study how people used to live. They sometimes use forensic techniques to identify ancient items and to find out information from human remains, such as how old the person was when they died, why they died and whether they had suffered from any injuries or diseases.

QUESTIONS

5 How is a paternity test carried out?

6 Why might a paternity test be used in an immigration case?

7 What type of industrial accident might a forensic scientist be asked to investigate?

Anastasia

Forensic scientists can help to solve many unusual problems.

In July 1917, the last Emperor of Russia, Czar Nicholas II (who was a distant relative of Prince Philip), his wife, five children and several of his servants were herded into a cellar and killed by a firing squad. The remains were buried and remained hidden for many years. Rumours circulated that one of Nicholas's daughters, named Anastasia, may have survived.

In the 1920s, a Polish woman known as Anna Anderson claimed that she was the missing Princess Anastasia. Her story captured the public imagination and has been made into a Hollywood film and a children's cartoon.

FIGURE 3: The daughters of Czar Nicholas II. Anastasia is third from the left.

QUESTIONS

8 When the bodies were discovered, forensic scientists were able to identify the Czar, his wife and three of his children using DNA evidence.

  a How did they prove that the remains they found were those of the Czar and his family?

  b The forensic scientists also proved that Anna Anderson was not Anastasia. How did they do this?

What techniques do forensic scientists use?

You will find out:
- Some techniques to identify and match evidence
- What is examined by forensic scientists
- That forensic evidence obtained may be used in law courts
- Why forensic evidence must be accurate and reliable

Broken glass

Windows are often broken to gain entry to cars, so thefts from cars often involve broken glass. Fragments of glass are very stable and can remain attached to pieces of clothing for a long time. **Forensic** scientists can use special techniques to analyse glass samples from a **suspect**'s clothes and from the crime scene to see whether they match. This can help to link a suspect to the **crime scene**.

How do forensic scientists match evidence from the crime scene?

Forensic scientists use the principle that every **contact** leaves a **trace**. Everyone who enters a crime scene will leave traces of **evidence** from them at the scene and pick up traces of evidence from the crime scene.

This trace evidence can be used to link suspects, **victims** or **witnesses** to a crime scene. Materials that can provide trace evidence often include:

- blood
- hairs
- paint
- fibres
- glass.

FIGURE 1: Forensic scientists analyse evidence from crime scenes.

Different forensic scientists have different areas of expertise and teams of forensic scientists often work together to solve complicated cases. Their evidence is used to produce a forensic science report. If the case goes to court, this report can be presented to help the court reach a decision about whether someone is guilty or innocent. The report is based on the evidence and the forensic scientist's opinions of what has happened, based on this evidence.

Forensic scientists use the principle that every contact leaves a trace

---

QUESTIONS

1 Explain the saying "every contact leaves a trace".
2 Why is trace evidence useful?
3 Name some materials that are typically analysed by forensic scientists.
4 Why do forensic scientists often work in teams?

...contact   ...crime scene   ...evidence   ...forensic

Why does a forensic scientist use different techniques?

Different techniques are used to analyse different types of evidence. Typically fingerprints are used to identify individuals, and blood can be analysed to test for the presence of alcohol, drugs or poisons.

The techniques chosen will depend upon the evidence available and the seriousness of the crime. A forensic scientist uses a range of techniques to try to answer questions, such as:

- Has a crime taken place?
- What is the identity of the victim?
- What is the identity of the suspect?
- How was the crime carried out?

Simply analysing the pattern of the blood stains at a crime scene can tell us a lot about what has happened. They can reveal the type of weapon that was used, how tall the attacker was, whether the attacker was left- or right-handed and how vicious the attack was.

What is the difference between accuracy and reliability?

An accurate result is one that is very close to the true value.

A reliable result is one that can be repeated. We can check that a result is reliable by repeating the test and seeing if the results are similar to each other. We can improve the reliability of a result by repeating the result several times and then calculating an average.

FIGURE 2: We can use a model to help us think about accuracy and precision. Here the archer is very accurate – she has hit the centre of the target.

FIGURE 3: This archer is precise but not very accurate. All three arrows have landed very close together but they haven't hit the centre of the target.

FIGURE 4: This archer is both precise and accurate. All three arrows have landed very close together near the centre of the target.

The Birmingham Six

In 1974, six men dubbed the Birmingham Six were found guilty of the Birmingham pub bombings, a devastating series of bombings that killed 21 people. The evidence against the men was largely based on the evidence from forensic tests and on the men's confessions, which they claimed had been forced from them. An important part of the forensic evidence showed that the men had handled organic nitrate compounds. These compounds are found in explosives like nitroglycerine.

It has since been found that the test used to establish that the men had contact with explosives also gives a positive result for contact with many household chemicals, and this forensic evidence against the men was dropped. In 1991, the Birmingham Six won their third appeal and their convictions were overturned.

FIGURE 5: The Birmingham Six celebrate their release from prison.

QUESTIONS

5 What are fingerprints used for?

6 What is an accurate result?

7 What is a reliable result?

QUESTIONS

8 Explain why it is important that forensic evidence is reliable.

9 Do you think we should convict people based largely on forensic evidence? Explain your answer.

Collecting evidence

You will find out:
- How forensic scientists avoid contaminating evidence from crime scenes
- About the sampling, storage and recording of forensic evidence

Why are photographs so important?

We use photographs to produce a permanent record of a **crime scene**. They are particularly useful if the case reaches court, because they help the people in the jury to be able to visualise the place where the crime has taken place.

FIGURE 1: Photographs can be used to record evidence that will not last.

Controlling the crime scene

FIGURE 2: Why are suspects detained?

The first officer arriving at a crime scene has a very important role. Their first task is to help anyone who has been hurt and then to talk to **witnesses** who may have seen what has happened. If the officer is able to identify any potential suspects, they are detained and removed from the crime scene so that they cannot return and **contaminate** the **evidence**.

Once this has been done, it is very important that the officer seals the area as quickly as possible. This helps to protect any evidence that the crime scene may hold. The area around the place where the crime has taken place is cordoned off with a ring of plastic tape to keep out members of the public.

The area is then examined. The number of investigating officers and forensic scientists entering the area is kept to a minimum and everyone entering the area has to wear protective clothing to prevent any evidence from being contaminated. Evidence from the scene is carefully sampled, stored and recorded.

FIGURE 3: The crime scene is cordoned off from the public.

QUESTIONS

1. On arriving at a crime scene, what is the first thing a police officer does?
2. Why are suspects detained?
3. Why is a crime scene cordoned off with plastic tape?
4. Why do investigators wear protective clothing?

...contaminate ...crime scene ...evidence ...identikit

How is evidence sampled?

Once a crime scene has been sealed off from the public, the **Scene of Crime Officers** (**SOCOs**) search the area for evidence. The SOCOs are specially trained civilians. Sometimes it is easy for us to recognise the pieces of evidence that will be important. However, on other occasions it might not be immediately obvious, so it is important that these officers do a thorough job. SOCOs use their training and experience to select the evidence to collect. Typical samples taken from a crime scene may include:

- broken glass
- fibres
- soil
- fingerprints
- blood.

Some crime scenes have to be searched very quickly. Evidence from outdoor areas can be damaged by wind or rain, so these areas will be a priority. Similarly, public areas like streets must also be searched quickly before they become contaminated.

How is evidence recorded?

Before any evidence is removed from a crime scene, it is **photographed** in position so that the entire crime scene can be reconstructed later. The evidence is also carefully labelled so that it can be identified correctly.

How is evidence stored?

Any evidence that has been collected from a crime scene must be stored carefully to stop it deteriorating or becoming contaminated. It is also important that we store evidence in a secure place so that there is no possibility of it being tampered with.

How can a witness help the police to find suspects?

Bystanders can provide vital information about suspects.

The **identikit** system can be used to build up a portrait of a suspect based on witness recollections. A large number of versions of each feature are shown to the witness, who can then pick out the version that most closely resembles the suspect they have seen. The result is a composite picture. These identikit pictures can be used to link known suspects to the crime scene or used to track down potential suspects. Computerised versions allow an even greater range of composites to be used. They also allow witnesses to adjust any of the features to get a better picture.

Why is the first officer arriving at a crime scene so important?

The first officer arriving at a crime scene can also be a very valuable witness. Some forensic evidence is very temporary. Things like unusual smells, or whether a door was open or closed may provide vital evidence. Even simple things like flushing a toilet can lose evidence and might even allow someone to get away with murder.

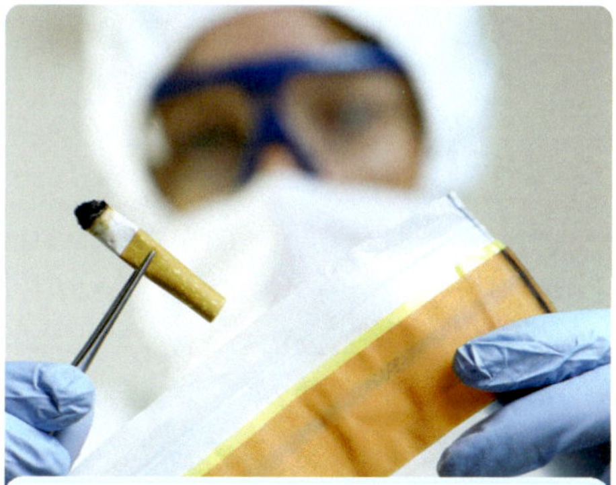

FIGURE 4: Why must evidence be stored carefully?

The O J Simpson trial

In 1994 the bodies of Nicole Brown Simpson and her close friend Ron Goldman were discovered at her Los Angeles home. They had been brutally murdered.

Suspicion immediately fell on Nicole's ex-husband O J Simpson. Simpson was a famous American footballer and movie star. After a hugely publicised trial that made headline news in America and Britain, Simpson was cleared of murder, mainly as a result of discrepancies in the forensic evidence.

QUESTIONS

9 When police officers arrived at Ms Brown Simpson's home they quickly realised what had happened. They used her telephone to report the double murder.

   a How might these police officers have damaged vital evidence?

   b What should the police officers have done?

QUESTIONS

5 Give an example of the type of evidence that can be collected from a crime scene.

6 Why should outdoor crime scenes be searched quickly?

7 Why is evidence photographed before it is removed from a crime scene?

8 Why must evidence from a crime scene be stored carefully?

...photographed   ...Scene of Crime Officers (SOCOs)   ...witnesses

Fingerprints

You will find out:

- How forensic scientists collect and record fingerprints
- How to reveal, lift and store fingerprints at a crime scene
- How to recognise different types of fingerprint patterns

Koala bears

Humans aren't the only animals to have **fingerprints**. Fingerprints are found in many climbing animals and help them to grip things. This koala's fingerprints help him to grip twigs and branches.

What are fingerprints?

Fingerprints are peaks of skin ridges. Everyone's fingerprint is different – even identical twins have slightly different fingerprints. The taking of fingerprints is the most commonly used forensic technique. Fingerprints left at a crime scene or on items of evidence can be used to identify suspects, victims and witnesses. The prints at crime scenes are carefully revealed, lifted and stored.

There are three types of fingerprint pattern:

- **Arch** – this is the least common type of print, where the skin ridges form wave type patterns.
- **Loop** – the skin ridges form loop type patterns.
- **Whorl** – this is the most common type of print, where the skin ridges form circle type patterns.

FIGURE 1: How do fingerprints help this koala bear?

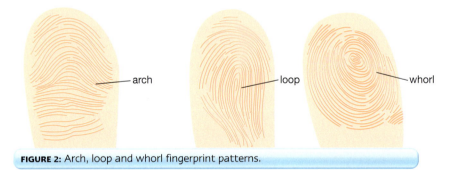

arch

loop

whorl

FIGURE 2: Arch, loop and whorl fingerprint patterns.

Everyone's fingerprint is different – even identical twins have slightly different fingerprints

---

QUESTIONS

1 What are fingerprints?
2 What is the most commonly used forensic technique?
3 Why are the fingerprints left at crime scenes useful?
4 What are the **three** types of fingerprint pattern?

How can fingerprints be left at a crime scene?

Latent or hidden prints are left accidentally at crime scenes. Occasionally, prints can be contaminated by blood or paint and this can make them even more visible. Windows are often used as the entrance or exit points of crime scenes. Fingerprints can also be left in soft materials like the putty around window frames.

How are fingerprints revealed, lifted and stored?

Most fingerprints are caused by sweat or grease from the fingertips being left on a surface. In the right light we can see these prints on surfaces like glass, but they do eventually dry out and in darker conditions they can be hard to see. The prints can be revealed using powder and a brush. The powder sticks to the grease in the fingerprint and makes it more visible. These prints can then be lifted using tape. The tape is placed over the print and, when it is removed, it lifts a copy of the print. The copy is covered with a layer of clear plastic for protection. The prints are then carefully stored.

FIGURE 3: Dusting for fingerprints at a crime scene.

How are a suspect's fingerprints taken?

A suspect's fingerprints are taken by placing the finger in ink and then onto paper. The prints are then photographed. Computers are used to compare these prints with prints taken from the crime scene. The computers can work out whether the two sets of prints came from the same finger. Fingerprint identifications are extremely reliable.

Can footprints be used to identify people?

Skin ridges are also found on the soles of the feet and footprints can also be used to identify people. The footprints of military air crew are sometimes recorded. If a plane crashes, it normally burns. The bodies of the crew can be unrecognisable and the fingerprints can be destroyed. The footprints, protected by socks and boots, are more likely to survive and can be used to identify the bodies.

QUESTIONS

5 What are latent fingerprints?
6 How are most fingerprints caused?
7 How are fingerprints revealed?
8 What are footprints?

How can fingerprints be used to catch criminals?

Juan Vucetich was the first person to catch a criminal using fingerprint evidence.

In 1892, Francisca Rojas was discovered with her throat cut, near the bodies of her two dead sons. Rojas recovered and claimed that they had been attacked by a neighbour.

However, when Vucetich examined the crime scene, he discovered Rojas' bloody fingerprints near the dead boys. He challenged Rojas and she immediately confessed, revealing that she had a secret lover who would only marry her if she got rid of her children.

QUESTIONS

9 Explain how Vucetich would have proved that Rojas was guilty of murdering her sons.

10 Rojas confessed her crimes and was found guilty. Imagine that you were a member of the jury. If she had not confessed, would you have been able to find her guilty? Explain your answer.

Hit and run

INVESTIGATION

Sarah has decided to investigate the scene of a road traffic accident involving a schoolboy called Luke for her assignment.

Following the accident, a police officer was sent to the scene. She cordoned off the area and interviewed a witness who described what she had seen.

This is what the witness said:
"It was a very hot afternoon. The driver was driving too fast. As the car came round the corner, he lost control. The car mounted the pavement and crashed into Luke. He was thrown into the air and landed in the road, badly hurt. The driver stopped, but when he saw Luke was not moving he drove away."

The witness stayed with Luke and phoned for an ambulance to take him to hospital. The witness thought the car might have been a red Vauxhall Corsa with an 2005 plate, but she couldn't see the driver clearly.

The police decided to follow up this lead. They checked the DVLA database to find out whether there were any red Corsas with 2005 plates registered to local people. One match was found. They visited the owner of this car. Its front bumper was damaged. The owner said the car had been damaged when he hit a cat that had run into the road.

Normally, evidence is removed from crime or accident scenes by specially trained Scene of Crime Officers (SOCOs) and then sent to special laboratories for analysis.

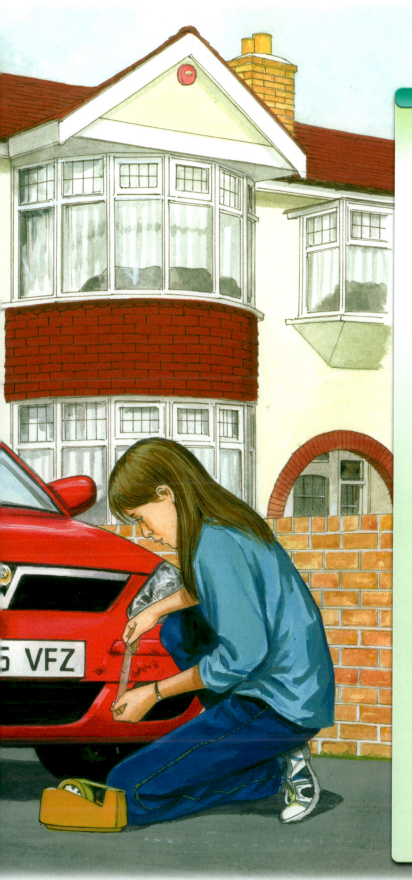

Here is Sarah's report:

I decided to study the scene of a hit-and-run accident because this is typical of the sort of crime that a forensic scientist is asked to investigate. Forensic evidence can be used to work out whether this red Corsa was involved in the accident.

> 1A.1 Sarah states a simple vocational application of her investigation. She could improve her mark by doing some research and using this to explain why her investigation is important.

After reading the witness's statement and examining the accident scene, I decided to collect paint and fibre samples from Luke's coat, which was left at the accident scene, and from the suspect's car.

Plan for collecting the evidence:
- Place adhesive tape over Luke's coat.
- Lift the tape so that the samples stick to the tape.
- Stick the tape onto a glass slide.
- Examine the slide using a microscope.
- Write down what any paint or fibre samples look like.
- Repeat these steps to examine the evidence from the suspect's car.

> 2B.1 Sarah has produced a plan for the investigation with a little help from her teacher. The plan is detailed enough to be followed by another person. To improve her mark, Sarah could work more independently and produce a more detailed plan for the investigation. When she examines the slide using the microscope, what is she looking for?

Hit and run

My teacher asked me to fill in this
risk assessment for my investigation.

Risk Assessment Form

DESCRIBE THE INVESTIGATION

Preparing and examing slides of paint samples and fibre samples.

WHAT ARE THE HAZARDS?

Glass slides could break.

WHAT ARE THE RISKS?

I could cut myself on a broken glass slide – medium risk.
Someone else could cut themselves on a broken glass slide – low risk.

HOW CAN THE RISK BE CONTROLLED?

I will make sure I am careful when I prepare the slide. When I am examining the slide using the microscope, I will put the slide on to the microscope, then move the stage to the top. I will then look through the eyepiece and move the stage down so I do not break the glass slide. If I drop the glass slide, I will use a dustpan and brush and clear it up straight away.

WHAT IS THE REMAINING RISK?

Low, provided I follow the lab rules carefully.

2B.2 Sarah has used the guidelines provided by her teacher to carry out a risk assessment for the investigation. She could improve her mark by carrying out the risk assessment independently.

The evidence

Fibre from Luke's coat	Fibre from the suspect's car
Lots of black wool	Grey cat's hair
Paint from Luke's coat	**Paint from the suspect's car**

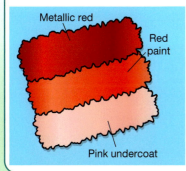

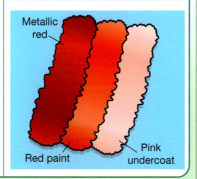

2C.1 Sarah has selected the appropriate equipment for the investigation with a little guidance from her teacher and has used it correctly and safely to carry out the plan to collect and record data accurately. To improve her work, Sarah could work more independently. She could also plan to repeat her measurements.

What it means

The paint samples match, so this shows me that the witness was probably right: Luke was likely to have been hit by a red Corsa with 2005 plates. But the fibres do not match. This means that this car probably did not hit Luke. If it had, I would expect to see fibres from Luke's coat transferred onto the car. The cat hair found on the suspect car's bumper confirms the car owner's story – the damage to the car was likely to have been done when the car hit a grey cat.

1D.1 Sarah has used the information collected from her investigation to draw some simple conclusions. Sarah could analyse her results in more detail. Are there any other cars that have the same paint details? If there are, the police might miss the car they are looking for.

How my investigation could be improved

I think this investigation could have been improved if I had taken more samples from the car and more samples from the clothes Luke was wearing.

I think my findings could be used to prove that the driver was not guilty, but the police should continue to look for a red Corsa.

2E.1 Sarah has evaluated her investigation and made a suggestion as to how to improve it.

2E.2 Sarah has suggested how the findings from her investigation could be used in the context of the forensic investigation. Sarah could improve her mark by evaluating her work more thoroughly:
- What were the strengths and weaknesses in her investigation?
- How could she collect more reliable and accurate evidence?

Fibres

You will find out:
- How fibres are collected from a crime scene
- How an electron microscope can be used to examine fibre samples

Cat hair

Hair is a naturally occurring type of **fibre**. Forensic scientists are able to identify the hair by examining it under a microscope. Animal hairs have characteristic scales that can be used to identify the animal they come from.

FIGURE 1: Cat hair can be recognised by the way that the scales on the hair overlap.

Why are fibres important?

Fibres are long, thin, flexible materials. Fabrics such as wool, cotton and linen are made from fibres that have been woven together. Today many synthetic fibres such as nylon and polyester are also available.

Fibres are often found at **crime scenes**. They are easily transferred during struggles between people. They are also extremely useful for identifying cars involved in hit-and-run incidents, where a car hits a pedestrian and then drives away. When the car hits someone, pieces of fibre from the person's clothes become attached to the car. Matching these fibres can **link** the car to the crime scene.

How are fibres collected?

Fibres are collected by placing **adhesive tape** onto the surface being tested and then carefully lifting the tape with the fibres now attached to it. The fibres can then be examined using a **microscope**. Different tapes with different amounts of stickiness can be used for different situations.

Fibres are long, thin, flexible materials

QUESTIONS

1 What are fibres?
2 How are fabrics made?
3 Explain the term hit-and-run accident.
4 How are fabrics collected from a crime scene?

...accurate   ...adhesive tape   ...crime scenes

How are electron microscopes used to identify fibres?

Forensic scientists use powerful equipment to identify samples. This equipment can give very **accurate** results with even very small samples.

Electron microscopes can be used to examine hair samples. Light microscopes are useful but they can only magnify objects about 1000 times. If we want to see very small things like the nucleus of an individual cell we require a magnification of 10 000 times or greater. Electron microscopes are much more powerful than light microscopes. They use beams of electrons to form an image of the surface of an object. Electrons have a much shorter wavelength than light rays. This gives us a much better resolution so we can see much smaller details. Electron microscopes can also be used to examine dust and crystals.

Why are some fibres more important than others?

The significance of a fibre matched to a crime scene will depend on how common the fibre is. Unusual fibres can provide strong evidence to link someone to a crime scene, but more common fibres such as white cotton will provide less convincing evidence.

How can different fibres be identified?

Natural fibres such as cotton or linen have distinctive features that can be identified under a microscope. Because of the way in which they are manufactured, synthetic fibres have a more uniform appearance, but they can be told apart by their melting point and solubility.

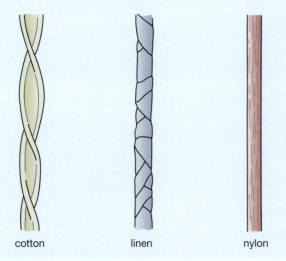

cotton   linen   nylon

FIGURE 2: Natural fibres are easier to identify.

QUESTIONS

5   Why are electron microscopes used?
6   Why do electron microscopes have better resolution than light microscopes?
7   Why will an unusual fibre be more useful than a common fibre?
8   How can synthetic fibres be identified?

EXAM HINTS AND TIPS

You must be able to explain how fibres are collected from a crime scene.

Fibre evidence

Between 1979 and 1981 more than twenty young people were murdered in Atlanta, Georgia. It appeared that a serial killer was targeting black young men and children.

As their bodies were discovered, forensic scientists used fibres removed from the victims' bodies to prove that there were links between the murders, but they were unable to identify the murderer. As many of the bodies were recovered from rivers, the police began to patrol the river banks, hoping to find a suspect. One team noticed a young black man named Wayne Williams dumping something into the river. They questioned and then released him when he claimed to be simply dumping rubbish in the river. When a body was recovered downstream from where Williams had been spotted two days later, he became the prime suspect. Forensic scientists examined fibres from Williams' clothes, home and car and found matches with the fibres found on the victims' bodies. Although Williams denied all the charges, he was found guilty on two counts of murder and sentenced to life imprisonment.

QUESTIONS

9   Describe how fibre evidence can be collected and matched to fibres from the victims' bodies.
10 Williams has always protested his innocence. Should we convict someone on evidence like this? How else could these fibres come to be found on the victims' bodies?

...fibre   ...link   ...microscope

Glass

You will find out:
- That glass fragments from a suspect can be matched with those from a crime scene
- How to measure the refractive index of a glass block
- How to measure the refractive index of glass fragments

Bullet-proof glass

Bullet-proof glass has recently been installed in the House of Commons following fears that terrorists might try to assassinate the Prime Minister. Normal glass does not offer protection from a gunman; the glass simply shatters as the bullet passes through. Bullet-proof glass consists of a layer of a tough plastic polycarbonate material sandwiched between layers of glass. This means that bullet-proof glass can withstand a round of bullets before breaking, and this should give security teams enough time to act.

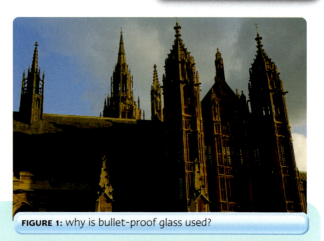

FIGURE 1: why is bullet-proof glass used?

Why is it important to be able to match glass samples?

Broken **glass** is often found at crime or accident scenes. Glass is easily **broken** and when it breaks, tiny shards of glass scatter over a large area. These small pieces of glass can be caught on pieces of clothing, embedded in the soles of shoes and even in the edges of tools. Glass is a very stable material, so pieces of glass can remain attached to these objects for a long time. Glass fragments are a very good way of **linking** a suspect to a crime scene.

Glass fragments are a very good way of linking a suspect to a crime scene

How can we identify different types of glass?

Have you noticed that when you place a spoon in a beaker of water, the teaspoon appears to bend at the point where it leaves the water? This is caused by a process called refraction. As light travels from the water (a more dense material) to air (a less dense material), it changes speed and bends. Different types of glass have different densities so they bend, or refract, light by slightly different amounts. This can be measured and used to match a sample of glass from a suspect to a sample taken from a crime scene.

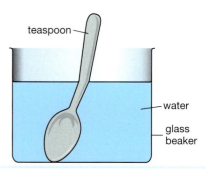

FIGURE 2: Why does this spoon appear to bend?

QUESTIONS

1 Why are glass fragments often found at crime scenes?
2 Why should a suspect's clothes be searched for glass?
3 How are forensic scientists able to match glass samples?
4 Why do different types of glass refract light by different amounts?

How can we measure how much a glass block refracts a ray of light?

We measure the amount a sample of glass **refracts** light by calculating the **refractive index** of the material. Different types of glass refract light by slightly different amounts and have slightly different refractive indexes.

Figure 3 shows what happens when a ray of light hits a glass block. A line labelled the normal is also shown. It is drawn at right angles to the edge of the glass block. The angle of incidence is the angle between the incident ray and the normal. The angle of refraction is the angle between the refracted ray and the normal.

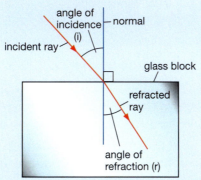

FIGURE 3: What happens when a ray of light hits a glass block?

How can we calculate the refractive index of a glass block?

There is a relationship between the angle that the incident ray hits the glass block and the angle that the ray is refracted.

The refractive index of a glass block is given by the sine of the angle of incidence (I) divided by the sine of the angle of refraction (R):

$$\text{refractive index} = \frac{\sin I}{\sin R}$$

The sine of an angle can be found using a calculator.

How can we measure the refractive index of glass shards?

Tiny pieces of glass are often found at crime scenes, so we must use a different method to find the refractive index of this glass.

The pieces of glass are placed in oil. As the oil is warmed up, the refractive index of the oil changes, and when the temperature of the oil reaches a point at which the refractive index of the oil is equal to the refractive index of the glass, the pieces of glass become almost invisible.

Forensic scientists know the refractive index of the oil at each temperature, so they are able to work out the refractive index of the glass sample from the temperature of the oil.

Different colours

When white light hits a prism, it is split into a spectrum by a process known as dispersion. When white light hits the prism, each different colour is refracted by a lightly different amount. Red light has the longest wavelength and is refracted least, while violet light has the shortest wavelength and is refracted most.

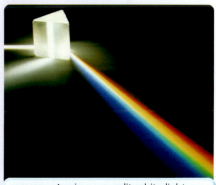

FIGURE 4: A prism can split white light into all the colours of the rainbow.

Because different wavelengths of light are refracted by different amounts, the wavelength of light used will affect the refractive index of a material. This can be shown by comparing the refractive index for a sample of glass using violet light and red light.

Refractive index using violet light: 1.528
Refractive index using red light: 1.515

QUESTIONS

5 Define the angle of incidence?

6 Define the angle of refraction?

Look at the figure on the right.

7 Calculate the sine of angle x.

8 Calculate the sine of angle y.

angle y
5.2 cm
3.5 cm
angle x
42.3°
4.0 cm

QUESTIONS

9 Give an approximate value for the refractive index of the glass sample using yellow light.

10 When measuring the refractive index of a material, why should the colour of light used also be recorded?

Marks left at crime scenes

You will find out:
- How forensic scientists can record the marks left at crime scenes
- How these marks can link objects and people to crime scenes
- How pollen grains, paint and bullets are identified

Pollen grains

Flowers contain a plant's reproductive system. The male organs, called stamens, produce pollen. Pollen grains from different plants have an amazing range of shapes, sizes and surface patterns. These can be used to identify the plant the pollen came from. Different pollens are around at different times of the year. Forensic scientists are particularly interested in recovering pollen grains from bodies that have been hidden for some time. The mixture of pollens, called the 'pollen signature', can be used to help identify when and where the crime took place.

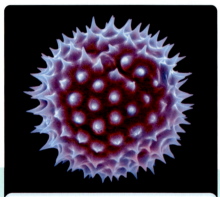

FIGURE 1: A pollen grain from a marigold flower.

Why are the marks left at crime scenes important?

A shoeprint, often called a **footprint**, left at a crime scene can be used to link a **suspect** to the scene. As a shoe becomes worn, the sole becomes scratched and these marks can be very distinctive. The size of the print and the particular print left by the sole of the shoe can also be useful. Vehicles can also leave traces at crime scenes. Again, the print left can be used to identify the type of **tyre** that has caused it. Typically shoes and tyres leave impressions in soft ground such as mud. Sometimes soil from the crime scene can be linked to soil obtained from a suspect's shoes or clothes. Soils are examined using a **polarising microscope**.

Forensic scientists can also use paint flecks to link a car to a crime scene such as a hit-and-run accident when a vehicle hits a pedestrian and then drives away.

Tools are often used during crimes. Tools like screwdrivers can be used to prise open windows and allow access to buildings. These tools can leave marks in soft material like the putty around windows. The edges of the tools will have tiny imperfections and they will leave a record of these in the marks they leave. Forensic scientists will photograph these marks or casts of these marks which they have made using plaster of Paris. These unique patterns can be used to link a particular tool to a crime scene.

As a shoe becomes worn the sole becomes scratched and these marks can be very distinctive

---

QUESTIONS

1. What is a shoeprint?
2. How are tyre prints used?
3. How can soil be used to link a suspect to a crime scene?

...cast ...comparison microscope ...footprint ...polarising microscope

How can forensic scientists identify the gun used at a crime scene?

When a bullet is loaded and fired from a gun, distinctive marks are left on the bullet. Scratches called **striation marks** are lines left on the bullet by tiny imperfections in the gun barrel. Forensic scientists can compare these striation marks to find out whether two bullets have been fired from the same gun.

The bullets are compared using a **comparison microscope**. This is a special type of microscope that allows two bullets to be viewed side by side through the same eyepiece. This allows the forensic scientist to see if there are any differences between the striation marks on the two bullets. If the striation marks are identical, the bullets must have been fired from the same gun. This can be used to link bullets removed from different crime scenes and may help investigators to make links between crimes that had previously been viewed as separate events. This technique can also be used to establish whether the gun has fired a particular bullet. This can be useful if police find a suspect who has a gun in their possession. A bullet is fired from the gun being tested into a tank of water. The bullet is then retrieved and examined. If the striation marks on this bullet match the marks on the bullet found at the crime scene, then the gun must have also fired the bullet from the crime scene.

How can paint be matched to a hit-and-run crime scene?

If a car hits someone and drives away, forensic scientists can help to work out what has happened from tiny specks of paint left from the car at the crime scene.

Today cars are painted in an enormous range of colours and finishes. Every year the paints used change as new colours become available and as fashions change. Typically a car is covered in several layers of paint, and each layer has a different composition. This can be used to identify the make, model and even year of the car involved in an accident. If a suspect has already been identified, then forensic scientists can check whether the sample from the crime scene matches the paint from the suspect's vehicle.

How are footprints recorded?

Forensic scientists often photograph the footprints left at crime scenes. A ruler is placed alongside the print so that the actual size of the print can be compared against a suspect's shoe. The prints may also be recorded by making a plaster of Paris **cast**. This method allows the forensic scientist to preserve the print with much greater detail, as even tiny marks and scratches are recorded. Tool and tyre prints can be recorded in a similar way.

FIGURE 2: How can a bullet be linked to a particular gun?

The campus killer

Between 1974 and 1978, serial killer Ted Bundy murdered at least 16 girls and young women. Many of these women were killed on university campuses. Ted Bundy was an unlikely serial killer; he was a popular, handsome lawyer with a psychology degree. He was also very careful; he carefully wiped down the crime scenes so that there was no fingerprint evidence. Bundy was eventually convicted largely on forensic evidence. A bite mark was found on the body of one of his young victims. Investigators noticed the bite on the girl's body, placed a ruler next to it and photographed the mark. Bundy was found guilty of murder and eventually executed.

QUESTIONS

8 Why were the bite marks photographed alongside a ruler?

9 Explain how forensic scientists would have been able to match Ted Bundy to the bite mark on the body.

QUESTIONS

4 What are the marks left on bullets called?

5 How are these marks caused?

6 How can a forensic scientist prove that a bullet has been fired by a particular gun?

7 Why are plaster of Paris casts used to record footprints?

Blood

You will find out:
- How to collect blood samples from a crime scene
- How blood typing can be used
- How human blood is identified
- About the composition of blood
- About the main blood groups

Luminol

If something that looks like **blood** is found at a crime scene, forensic scientists will spray the substance with a chemical called luminol. If blood is present, the luminol glows a green-blue colour. The more blood that is present, the more it glows. Unfortunately, luminol can give false results; it also glows when sprayed on horseradish.

FIGURE 1: Testing for blood at a crime scene.

Why is blood important to a forensic scientist?

Blood is often found at the scene of violent crimes such as murders, rapes or assaults. Blood samples can also be used to identify victims, suspects and witnesses to these crimes. Even when someone tries to clean up a crime scene, **traces** of blood can remain hidden between floor boards or beneath pipes. These blood stains can help us to work out what really happened at a crime scene. This helps us to tell whether witnesses are telling the truth or lying about the events.

What is blood?

Blood is a very important substance. It supplies the cells in the body with oxygen and glucose and removes carbon dioxide and lactic acid. If we are injured, we can lose blood. If someone loses half of their blood, they will die. Blood consists of:

- **plasma** - red blood **cells** - white blood cells - **platelets**

What are blood groups?

There are several ways of classifying **blood groups**. The most popular one used in this country is the ABO system. Blood can be split into four groups:

- Group A - Group B - Group AB - Group O

Blood is often found at the scene of violent crimes such as murders, rapes or assaults

Your blood group depends on the genes that you have inherited from your parents.

Blood group tests can be used to classify blood samples. These tests are cheap and fast and can be carried out at the crime scene. Although they do not identify an individual, if the blood group of a suspect does not match blood found at the crime scene, that particular line of enquiry can quickly be discounted, so these tests can be very useful.

> **QUESTIONS**
>
> 1 Who can blood samples be used to identify?
> 2 What does blood do?
> 3 What does blood consist of?
> 4 Name the **four** blood groups.

...antibodies ...antigens ...blood ...blood groups

Why are blood groups important?

Around the world, different populations have different frequencies of blood groups. In the UK, most people have blood group O or A (see table 1).

In fact, most people in the world have blood group O and anyone can receive blood from blood group O if they need a blood transfusion. But if you tried to give someone with blood group O some group A blood, it could be fatal. This is because of the **antibodies** present in the blood plasma.

Antigens are foreign bodies. Antibodies are produced to protect the body from antigens.

- Blood from blood group A has A antigens covering the red blood cells and anti-B antibodies in the plasma.
- Blood group B has B antigens covering the red blood cells and anti-A antibodies in the plasma.
- Blood group AB has A and B antigens covering the red blood cells and no antibodies in the plasma.
- Blood group O has no antigens covering the red blood cells and anti-A and anti-B antibodies in the plasma.

Blood group	% of UK population
O	44
A	42
B	10
AB	4

TABLE 1: Percentages of people with each blood group in the UK.

How can we test whether a blood sample is human?

Forensic scientists can test whether a blood sample comes from a human being by adding a chemical called an antiserum. If the blood is human, a cloudy precipitate is formed. Forensic scientists can also test which blood group a sample is from.

The precipitin test

This test can be used to identify whether blood comes from a human or from another animal. The test was first used to identify whether blood came from chickens.

When antibodies mix with the correct antigen, a precipitate is formed. In the first test, protein from the egg of a chicken was injected into a rabbit. The protein from the chicken egg was a foreign body or antigen to the rabbit. The rabbit produces antibodies to protect itself from the antigen. This is called an antiserum. The antiserum is collected from the rabbit and then mixed with blood from the chicken. The antibodies in the antiserum react with the antigens in the chicken blood to form a cloudy precipitate called precipitin. This method was quickly adapted to test for the presence of human blood.

QUESTIONS

5 What is the least common blood group in the UK?
6 Why could blood group O be known as the 'universal donor'?
7 What are antigens?
8 Why are antibodies produced?

QUESTIONS

9   How could you make antiserum to prove that a blood sample came from a cat?
10 Explain why it is important that forensic evidence is reliable.

...cells ...plasma ...platelets ...traces

Forgery

INVESTIGATION

Gethin has decided to investigate a case of some forged tickets in his assignment.

The police were called to the football ground at 2.30 pm. The staff at the turnstile had noticed that a number of people had tried to use forged tickets to enter the ground. The match had been sold out for weeks, so these people had been turned away and many were very upset. The police interviewed two friends who had arrived at the ground with forged tickets. They said they had bought the tickets outside the ground from a man they had not met before. They pointed him out to the police. The man claimed he was waiting for his friends. The police found that he had six forged tickets in his pocket. He claimed these were for his friends and denied having sold tickets to anyone else. When the police visited the man's home, they found a computer and printer in his bedroom. Gethin has decided to help collect and analyse the evidence.

Here is Gethin's report:

I decided to study the evidence in this case because this is the sort of crime that a forensic scientist is asked to investigate. Forensic evidence plays an important part in many police cases. I hope to find out whether the suspect handled any of the other forged tickets, which he is denying, and whether the printer in his bedroom was used to produce the tickets, which he is also denying.

I have decided to investigate how fingerprint evidence can be used to check whether the man had handled the tickets, and chromatography to find out whether the ink from the printer in the man's house matches the ink used to make the forged tickets. Fingerprint evidence is very important, because the fingerprints left at crime scenes and on pieces of evidence help the police to identify suspects and witnesses. Chromatography can be used to work out the number of components in a mixture. The technique works because different components have different solubilities. It can also be used to work out whether two samples of ink are the same. The technique of chromatography is very important in forensic science. It can be used to identify whether blood samples contain alcohol, drugs or even poisons.

3A.1 Gethin has researched and explained the significance of the techniques that he is going to use.

Gethin writes, "I have decided to collect fingerprints from one of the forged tickets and from the suspect to see if they match. I am also going to carry out a chromatography experiment to see if the ink on the forged ticket matches the ink from the suspect's printer."

Plan for the fingerprint evidence

- I am going to use powder and a brush to reveal the prints on the ticket. The powder sticks to the grease in the fingerprints and makes them easier to see.
- I will then place some clear tape over each print.
- I will lift the tape carefully and stick it onto a microscope slide.
- I will then take fingerprints from the suspect, the victim who was sold the ticket and the lady at the turnstile who handled the ticket. I will do this by asking them to place their fingers onto an ink pad and then placing them onto a microscope slide.
- I will examine the prints from the ticket against the prints from the people in my investigation. I need to see whether the prints come from the same person.

Plan for the ink evidence

- I will get two pieces of filter paper and cut them into rectangles.
- I will then use a ruler and pencil and draw a line exactly 0.5 cm from the bottom of my paper.
- I will put a drop of ink from the suspect's home in the middle of the pencil line on one piece of paper.
- I will use a moist cotton bud to take a sample of ink from the forged ticket and place it in the middle of the pencil line on the other piece of paper.
- I will get two beakers and place water to a depth of 0.2 cm in each beaker.
- I will then place one piece of paper in each beaker.
- When the water reaches the top of the beaker, I will remove each of the pieces of paper.
- I will measure the distance the ink has moved and the distance the water has moved.
- I will do each investigation three times.

3B.1 Gethin has worked independently to produce his plan. The plan is detailed enough to be followed by another person

Forgery

STUDENT'S COMMENTARY

My teacher helped me to fill in this risk assessment for my investigation.

Risk Assessment Form

WHAT ARE YOU DOING?

I am using a microscope and then doing a chromatography experiment.

WHAT ARE THE HAZARDS?

Are you using any dangerous chemicals?   Yes / (No)

Are you using any dangerous equipment?   Yes / (No)

Other hazards: *I could drop something.*

IS THE RISK LOW / (MEDIUM) / HIGH?

WHAT COULD YOU DO IF SOMETHING WENT WRONG?

I would tell my teacher straight away and not touch the glass myself.

> 1B.2 Gethin has carried out a risk assessment but the form he used had very clear guidelines. He could improve his mark by carrying out the risk assessment more independently.

The fingerprint evidence

Fingerprint from the ticket	Fingerprint from the suspect	Fingerprint from the victim	Fingerprint from staff at football ground

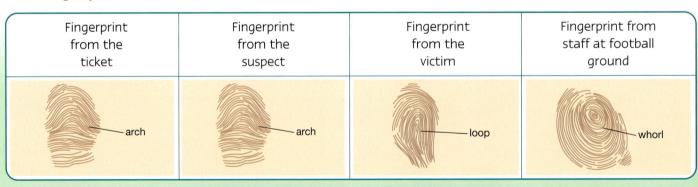

arch — arch — loop — whorl

The ink evidence

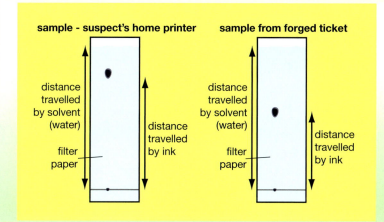

sample - suspect's home printer

distance travelled by solvent (water)

filter paper

distance travelled by ink

sample from forged ticket

distance travelled by solvent (water)

filter paper

distance travelled by ink

I have calculated the Rf value for the experiments.

This is given by the distance the ink has moved divided by the distance the solvent has moved.

	Sample from suspect's home	Sample from forged ticket
Run 1	Distance solvent moved = 10.0 cm Distance ink moved = 7.8 cm	Distance solvent moved = 10.0 cm Distance ink moved = 6.6 cm
Run 2	Distance solvent moved = 10.0 cm Distance ink moved = 7.9 cm	Distance solvent moved = 10.0 cm Distance ink moved = 6.4 cm
Run 3	Distance solvent moved = 10.0 cm Distance ink moved = 7.7 cm	Distance solvent moved = 10.0 cm Distance ink moved = 6.5 cm

	Rf value of sample from suspect's home	Rf value of sample from forged ticket
Run 1	0.78	0.66
Run 2	0.79	0.64
Run 3	0.77	0.65
Average	0.78	0.65

What it means

The fingerprints from the suspect appear to match the fingerprints on the ticket. This tells me that the suspect has handled the forged tickets, so he was not telling the truth. But the ink from the suspect's home does not match the ink from the forged tickets, so the printer was not used to produce the forged tickets.

How my investigation could be improved

I have tried to look at the fingerprints using a normal microscope, but it is difficult to compare the print from the ticket and that from the suspect. I think it would be better to compare the prints using a comparison microscope, so I can be sure they are the same. A comparison microscope would let me see both prints side by side.

I think I would ask the police to re-interview the suspect, tell him that we know he handled the forged tickets and ask him to tell us the truth about where they came from.

DNA

You will find out:
- That DNA can be extracted from blood, semen and saliva
- How DNA profiling works
- How DNA is inherited
- That DNA is found in the nucleus of cells

Mummies, brothers and sisters

Ancient Egypt was a highly developed civilisation. The country was ruled by kings called pharaohs. Egyptians believed that after people died they moved on to the afterlife, where they would still need their bodies. So when an important person like a pharaoh died, they deliberately tried to preserve their body using a technique called mummification. Historians studying manuscripts from these times were puzzled over records that seemed to suggest that some marriages took place between brothers and sisters. Scientists have studied the DNA from some of these mummies to try and resolve the issue. They found that records were indeed correct and that marriages between brothers and sisters did take place.

What is DNA?

Traditional laboratory methods of analysis can be quite slow and require a large amount of the sample to be available. Today, the development of a range of instrumental methods that are faster, more accurate, more sensitive and require smaller amounts of sample have revolutionised our ability to identify chemicals. **Deoxyribonucleic acid** or DNA is found in the nucleus of cells.

DNA can be extracted from blood, semen or saliva samples. **Blood** is often found at the scene of violent crimes, semen can be found at the scene of sexual assaults and saliva can be found on everything from cigarette butts to glasses.

DNA is extracted from the other materials in the sample and then fragments of the DNA are analysed using a technique called **electrophoresis**.

DNA is a long spiral-shaped molecule that carries **genetic** information. We can think of it as a set of instructions for making you. Your DNA is set at the moment of conception and stays the same throughout your life. Half of your DNA is inherited from your mum and half is inherited from your dad.

Although your DNA is very similar to that of your parents, brothers, sisters and other relatives, because nearly every person's DNA is unique it can be used to identify people. In fact, only **identical twins** have exactly the same DNA.

DNA can also be used to prove whether people are related or not. DNA profiling is used to identify suspects, witnesses and victims from evidence left at the crime scene.

FIGURE 1: DNA evidence helps us to work out how people are related to each other.

FIGURE 2: A DNA sample.

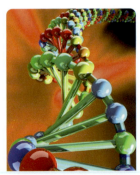

FIGURE 3: Your DNA carries the genetic instructions to make you.

> ### QUESTIONS
>
> 1 Where is DNA found?
> 2 Where can DNA be extracted from?
> 3 Where does a person's DNA come from?
> 4 How can DNA be used to link a person to a crime scene?

...blood   ...deoxyribonucleic acid (DNA)   ...DNA profiling

How does DNA profiling work?

Only a tiny proportion of DNA varies from one person to another. In **DNA profiling**, specific regions of the DNA that vary from person to person are scanned. The technique codes the person's genes into a series of numbers. The codes from different samples can then be compared. The more regions that are scanned, the more likely it is that any match found is correct, but the more expensive and time-consuming the test will be.

Fragments of DNA are separated by a process called electrophoresis. The fragments all have a negative charge but differ in length. When they are placed in an electric field, the shorter fragments move faster and can be separated from the longer fragments.

How do DNA databases help to solve crimes?

DNA databases store DNA profiles from known criminals, possible suspects in current cases and sometimes from people who have been reported missing.

If the DNA profiles match samples taken from a crime scene, this can help to link that person to the crime scene.

The databases can also be used to link several different incidents to one person if the samples from different crime scenes match. This can help the police find links between crimes, which may help them to identify the person involved.

DNA databases can also be used to find near matches. So, if a DNA sample does not match but is quite close to one found at a crime scene, the police could investigate the possibility that a close relative of the individual, such as a brother, may have been at the crime scene.

Databases are used to store vast quantities of information. Examples of information stored include:

- dental and medical records
- descriptions of missing people
- fingerprints
- lists of stolen goods.

The information in databases can be searched to find matches that can link suspects to a crime scene or to eliminate a suspect from an investigation.

What are the problems with DNA profiling?

Even though a person's genetic profile might match the genetic profile from a crime scene, this does not mean that the person is definitely guilty. Investigators must also consider other sources of evidence. If the DNA evidence backs up the other evidence, it can be quite compelling.

Some people also claim that it is so easy to contaminate DNA evidence during collection, analysis or storage that it is often unreliable.

FIGURE 4: DNA profiling can be used to compare one sample of DNA with another.

How can forensic scientists identify twins?

There are two types of twins:

- Fraternal twins are formed when two different eggs are fertilised by two different sperm. Fraternal twins are no more genetically similar than other pairs of siblings. They share about 50% of the same genes. Each twin has its own unique DNA which can be used to identify them.

- Identical twins are formed when a fertilised egg splits into two embryos. Each twin has the same DNA, so they cannot be told apart by DNA testing. However, although DNA sets the pattern for the fingerprints, they develop slightly differently in each individual. This means that although the prints are very similar, they are not identical, and this can be used to tell identical twins apart.

QUESTIONS

5 How does DNA profiling work?

6 How can a DNA database help to catch criminals?

7 If DNA profiles match, are they definitely from the same person?

8 When could DNA evidence be contaminated?

QUESTIONS

9 Can you think of any occasions when it could be a disadvantage to police officers that identical twins have the same DNA?

...electrophoresis   ...genetic   ...identical twins

Ionic compounds

You will find out:
- That chromatography can be used to separate mixtures
- About the structure and properties of ionic compounds
- Why ionic compounds dissolve in water

Counterfeit currency

The production of counterfeit currency is a major problem in many countries.

Forensic scientists use a technique called chromatography to identify the ink used to make forged notes. This can be used to find links between forged notes and can help the police to track down the counterfeiters.

FIGURE 1: How can forensic scientists identify the inks used to make counterfeit bank notes?

What is the structure of an ionic compound?

Once Scene of Crime Officers have collected evidence from a crime scene it is sent to the laboratory for analysis. Forensic scientists often want to **identify** the chemicals present in these samples. Many of these chemicals contain **ions**.

Although scientists originally thought that **atoms** could not be split into anything smaller, we now know that each atom actually consists of even tinier particles. These are called protons, neutrons and electrons.

At the centre of an atom is its nucleus. The nucleus consists of protons and neutrons. The nucleus is surrounded by shells of electrons. We call the protons, neutrons and electrons **sub-atomic** particles.

All atoms have equal numbers of protons and electrons, so they have no overall charge. An ion is an atom that has gained or lost electrons so that it becomes **charged**. When metal atoms form ions, they lose electrons. Metal ions always have a **positive** charge.

When non-metal atoms form ions, they gain electrons. Non-metal ions always have a **negative** charge.

Ionic compounds consist of many ions, which form a giant structure in which the positive ions and negative ions are placed alternately.

The ionic compound sodium chloride consists of alternate sodium and chloride ions and can be represented by the formula NaCl.

Strong forces of attraction act in all directions to hold all the ions together. We call these electrostatic forces of attraction between the oppositely charged particles ionic bonds.

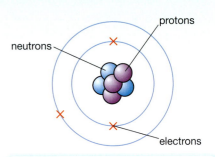

FIGURE 2: Atomic structure.

What are the properties of ionic compounds?

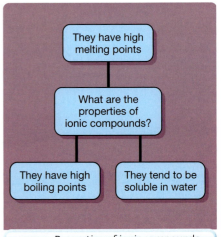

FIGURE 3: Properties of ionic compounds.

QUESTIONS

1 What is an ionic bond?
2 Why do metal atoms form positive ions?
3 Why do non-metal atoms form negative ions?

...atoms ...charged ...identity ...ions

Why do ionic substances have high melting points and boiling points?

We know that ionic compounds form giant ionic structures. In these structures, there are lots of strong ionic bonds. A great deal of energy is required to overcome the forces of attraction between the ions, so ionic compounds will only melt and boil at high temperatures. In fact, most ionic compounds will only melt at temperatures above 500 °C.

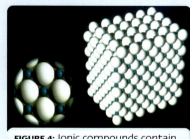

FIGURE 4: Ionic compounds contain lots of strong bonds.

Water as a solvent

Solvents are liquids that dissolve solutes to form solutions. Water is very good at dissolving ionic substances like salts, but not good at dissolving covalently bonded substances like fats or oils. Solubility is used to measure the maximum amount of a solute that will dissolve in a given amount of solvent (usually 100 g) at a particular temperature.

Different substances have different solubilities. Solubility also changes with temperature. This graph shows how the solubility of copper sulfate and potassium nitrate changes as the temperature increases. Notice how copper sulfate becomes slightly more soluble, while there is a very big increase in the solubility of potassium nitrate. Solids tend to become more soluble as the temperature increases.

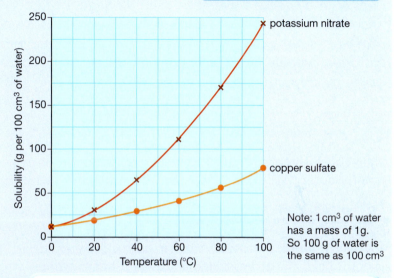

Note: 1 cm³ of water has a mass of 1g. So 100 g of water is the same as 100 cm³

FIGURE 5: A graph comparing the solubility of copper sulfate and potassium nitrate at different temperatures.

How does chromatography work?

Chromatography is a fast, cheap and powerful way of working out how many components are present in a mixture.

In thin layer chromatography (TLC), a plate is made by covering a glass or plastic slide with a layer of silica and zinc sulfide. Zinc sulfide fluoresces in ultraviolet light. A small sample of the chemical to be tested is placed at the bottom of the plate. The plate is then placed in a small amount of solvent. As the solvent moves up the plate, the components in the sample also move up the plate. Different components have different solubilities and so move different distances up the plate. As soon as the solvent reaches the top, the plate is removed. Ultraviolet light is shone onto the plate, which fluoresces, apart from the places where the components have reached. The number of components in the sample is shown by the number of marks on the plate.

Paper chromatography can be used to separate mixtures of different coloured inks.

QUESTIONS

4   What do we call a mixture of a solvent and a solute?
5   Would you expect the salt potassium chloride to dissolve well in water?
6   Why do we often measure how much solute will dissolve in 100 g of water?
7   How much copper sulfate dissolves in 100 g of water at 60 °C?

Poisoning problems

In the UK around 6000 people are killed by poisons every year. If the police believe that someone may have been deliberately or accidentally poisoned, they will ask forensic scientists to investigate samples of blood and liver from the victim.

QUESTIONS

8   **a** Describe how a forensic scientist would carry out thin layer chromatography on the sample.

b A bottle of a poison is found near the body. How could the forensic scientist use TLC to prove that the poison in the bottle is present in the tissues of the body of the victim?

Covalent compounds

You will find out:

● That when atoms share pairs of electrons, they form covalent bonds
● The names and formulae of some simple covalent substances
● How to test for the compounds carbon dioxide, glucose and ethanol

Poisons

Poisons are substances that can cause illness or even death in people and other animals. They have been used throughout history in murders, executions, assassinations and suicides. Some poisons can be extracted from plants, for example hydrogen cyanide is found in bitter almonds. Hydrogen cyanide is a deadly poison that contains covalent bonds. It kills people by stopping the cells in the body from being able to use oxygen.

Why do non-metal atoms form covalent bonds?

When non-metal atoms react together, both atoms need to gain **electrons** to get a full outer shell. They can only get this structure by **sharing** outer electrons.

What is a covalent bond?

A **covalent bond** is formed when two atoms share electrons. This shared pair of electrons holds the atoms together. Covalent bonds are very strong.

Organic compounds come from living substances and they all contain the element carbon. These compounds contain covalent bonds.

How do we represent covalent bonds?

Covalent bonding occurs in **simple molecules** and in giant covalent structures. Simple molecules are small groups of atoms held together by strong covalent bonds.

Molecules of **compounds** are formed when two or more different types of atom are joined together by shared pairs of electrons.

Examples of simple molecules include:

■ **carbon dioxide**, CO_2 ■ **water**, H_2O ■ **ethanol**, C_2H_5OH ■ **glucose**, $C_6H_{12}O_6$

Molecules of the compound water consist of one oxygen atom and two hydrogen atoms. The atoms in a water molecule are held together by covalent bonds. The covalent bonds in a water molecule can be represented by a line drawn between the oxygen atom and the hydrogen atoms as we can see in figure 2. Scientists can carry out special tests to find out if carbon dioxide, glucose or ethanol are present.

FIGURE 1: Poisons can harm or even kill people.

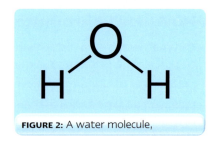

FIGURE 2: A water molecule.

What are simple molecules like?

Properties of simple molecules include:

■ They have low melting points and boiling points and are often liquids or gases at room temperature.

■ They are usually insoluble in water, although they may dissolve in other liquids.

QUESTIONS

1 Name the element found in all organic molecules.
2 What is a covalent bond?
3 Describe the bonding in a water molecule.
4 Give the formula for ethanol.

...carbon dioxide ...compounds ...covalent bond ...electrons ...ethanol

Why do simple molecules have low melting points and boiling points?

Although many simple molecular substances are liquids or gases at room temperature, we know that a few, like sulfur, are solids with low melting points.

Solid simple molecules like sulfur have a regular crystalline structure. Although there are very strong **forces of attraction** within each molecule, there are only weak forces of attraction between molecules.

How can we test for the presence of carbon dioxide?

We can test a gas to find out whether it is carbon dioxide by bubbling the gas through a solution of calcium hydroxide, which is commonly known as limewater. If carbon dioxide is present, it reacts with the calcium hydroxide to form insoluble calcium carbonate and the solution becomes cloudy. The reaction can be summed up by the equation:

$$\text{calcium hydroxide} + \text{carbon dioxide} \rightarrow \text{calcium carbonate} + \text{water}$$
$$Ca(OH)_{2(aq)} + CO_{2(g)} \rightarrow CaCO_{3(s)} + H_2O_{(l)}$$

How can we test for the presence of glucose?

We can test for the presence of glucose in a solution using Benedict's solution. Benedict's solution is a blue solution that contains Cu^{2+} ions.

Glucose is a reducing sugar. If glucose is present, it reduces the Cu^{2+} ions to Cu^+ ions and a red precipitate is seen:

$$Cu^{2+}_{(aq)} \rightarrow Cu^+_{(s)}$$

How can we test for the presence of ethanol?

Ethanol is a type of alcohol and is found in alcoholic drinks like beer and wine.

If a police officer thinks that a driver has been drinking alcohol, he or she will ask the driver to blow into a breathalyser. Their breath is then bubbled through a mixture containing potassium chromate (VI). If there is alcohol in the driver's breath, it reacts with the potassium chromate (VI) to form chromium sulfate.

As the reaction happens there is a colour change – potassium chromate (VI) is orange, while chromium sulfate is green. The amount of colour change can be used to monitor the reaction. This means that the amount of colour change can be used to work out the amount of alcohol in the driver's breath and therefore the level of alcohol in the blood.

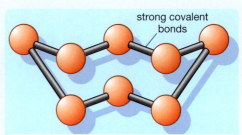
FIGURE 3: There are strong bonds between the sulfur atoms in each molecule.

strong covalent bonds

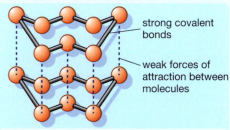
FIGURE 4: There are much weaker forces of attraction between sulfur molecules.

strong covalent bonds

weak forces of attraction between molecules

The effects of alcohol

Alcohol is a depressant. It slows down people's reactions and affects their judgement. There are strict laws to prevent people who have been drinking too much alcohol from driving vehicles.

FIGURE 5: Someone taking a breathalyser test.

QUESTIONS

9 Suggest why there are strict laws to prevent people who have been drinking too much alcohol from driving vehicles.

10 The results of breath tests are not admissible in courts. If a person tests positive in a breath test, they are asked to give a blood or urine sample. Suggest why the results of a breath test are not admissible in court but the results of a blood or urine test are.

QUESTIONS

5 Describe the bonding within sulfur molecules and between sulfur molecules.
6 What is the chemical test for the gas carbon dioxide?
7 We can test for the presence of glucose using Benedict's solution. Why does Benedict's solution change colour if sugar is present?
8 Name a type of alcohol.

Chemical tests

You will find out:
- How we can use flame tests to identify some metal ions
- How to use sodium hydroxide solution to detect some metal ions
- How to test for the presence of chloride and sulfate ions
- How carbonate ions react with acids

Lead poisoning

Lead is a soft metal that is poisonous to people. In the past, lead has been used in paints, and older houses may still contain lead-based paints. Lead poisoning can cause nausea, brain damage or even coma. Young children are particularly at risk because lead-based paints have a sweet taste and some young children lick or suck painted areas like windowsills. High levels of lead have also been found in cosmetics containing kohl imported from India and Pakistan.

FIGURE 1: Kohl is used in many cosmetics.

What happens in flame tests?

Scientists often need to **identify** the metal ions in compounds. For example, a scientist might want to analyse the paint on a child's toy to find out if it contains lead.

Can you remember seeing the different coloured lights made when fireworks explode? When some metal salts in fireworks are heated they release different coloured lights:

- Sodium salts contain Na^+ ions and produce yellow-orange flames.
- Potassium salts contain K^+ ions and produce lilac flames.
- Calcium salts contain Ca^{2+} ions and produce brick-red flames.
- Copper salts contain Cu^{2+} ions and produce blue-green flames.

How can we use sodium hydroxide solution to identify metals?

Some metal ions can be identified by observing their reaction with sodium hydroxide solution:

- **Solutions** containing Ca^{2+} ions give white **precipitates**.
- Solutions containing Cu^{2+} ions give pale blue precipitates.
- Solutions containing Fe^{2+} ions give grey-green precipitates.
- Solutions containing Fe^{3+} ions give fox-brown precipitates.

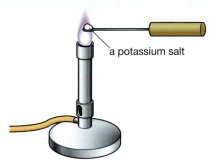

a potassium salt

FIGURE 2: Flame tests can be used to identify metals in compounds.

Scientists often need to identify the metal ions in compounds

QUESTIONS

1   Why do fireworks give out light of different colours?
2   What is the colour of the light given out when potassium salts are heated?
3   An unknown metal salt produces a green flame when heated. Which metal is in the unknown salt?
4   If you add sodium hydroxide solution to a solution containing iron (II) ions what would you see?

...flame tests   ...identify   ...insoluble

How is a flame test carried out?

Flame tests are a powerful way of identifying the metal ions present in a compound. First the sample is placed on a watch glass. A very clean platinum wire is dipped into concentrated hydrochloric acid and then into the sample. The wire is then put into a hot, blue Bunsen burner flame. This test is particularly useful for identifying Group 1 and Group 2 metal ions in compounds.

When a metal ion is heated in a Bunsen flame, it uses the heat energy to promote an electron from its usual energy level to an excited energy level. When the electron falls back down, light is given out. The colour of the light given out can be used to identify the metal ion in the compound.

FIGURE 3: Heat energy can be used to promote an electron to a higher energy level.

Does a sample contain sulfate ions?

We can find out whether a sample contains sulfate ions by dissolving it in water and adding dilute hydrochloric acid followed by a few drops of dilute barium chloride solution. If the sample contains sulfate ions, a white precipitate of barium sulfate is formed. Barium sulfate is a white insoluble solid.

Does a sample contain chloride ions?

We can find out whether a sample contains any chloride ions by dissolving the sample in water and adding dilute nitric acid followed by a few drops of dilute silver nitrate solution. If chloride ions are present, a white precipitate forms.

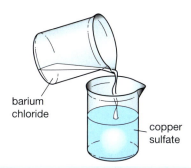

FIGURE 4: Copper sulfate solution contains copper ions and sulfate ions. The sulfate ions react with the barium ions in barium chloride to form a precipitate of barium sulfate.

Does a sample contain carbonate ions?

We can find out whether a sample contains carbonate ions by adding dilute acid. If carbonate ions are present, they react with the acid to form the gas carbon dioxide, which turns limewater cloudy.

Does a solution contain lead (II) ions?

We can find out whether a sample contains lead (II) ions by dissolving it in water and adding potassium iodide solution. If the sample contains lead (II) ions a yellow precipitate of lead iodide is formed. Lead iodide is a yellow **insoluble** solid.

How do we test the pH of a solution?

We can find out whether a solution is acidic, neutral or alkaline by testing it with **Universal Indicator** paper. This turns different colours depending on the type of solution being tested. Strong acids turn it red, neutral solutions turn it green and strong akalis turn it purple. Some solutions must be filtered before further tests can be carried out. We can find out whether a soil sample is acidic by dissolving the soil in water, filtering it and then testing it with Universal Indicator paper.

Identifying a dangerous chemical

Scientists sometimes have to carry out a series of tests to confirm the identity of a compound.

A blue solution was placed into someone's drink. They became very unwell and were admitted to hospital. To discover the identity of the solution, scientists took two samples. To the first sample they added sodium hydroxide and a pale blue precipitate was formed. To the second sample, they added a solution of barium chloride and a white precipitate was formed.

QUESTIONS

9 Identify the metal ions in the blue solution.

10 Identify the other ions in the blue solution.

11 Give the name and formula of the compound in the blue solution.

QUESTIONS

5 Why must the wire used in a flame test be very clean?

6 How is a flame test used to identify a metal ion?

7 Which gas is produced when a metal carbonate reacts with acid?

8 How is a precipitate formed?

Burglary

INVESTIGATION

Ed has decided to investigate the scene of a burglary for his assignment.

Mrs Shah was sitting in her garden, enjoying the sunny weather. She had left a window in the sitting room open to try and keep the house cool. When she came into the house, she noticed that the front door was open. When she went into the front room, she saw that the vase of sunflowers on the windowsill had been disturbed and her television and DVD player were missing. Someone had got through the window, burgled her house and then escaped through the front door. She called the police, who arrived and interviewed Mrs Shah. They sent for a Scene of Crime Officer to search the house for evidence. There were no fingerprints, but the officer found a short brown hair and some pollen from the sunflowers on the carpet. The following day, the police drove around the area and spotted a man behaving suspiciously. He had a pair of gloves in his pocket, even though it was very hot. He also had a yellow mark on the side of his jeans. The police thought he might be involved in the burglary at Mrs Shah's house.

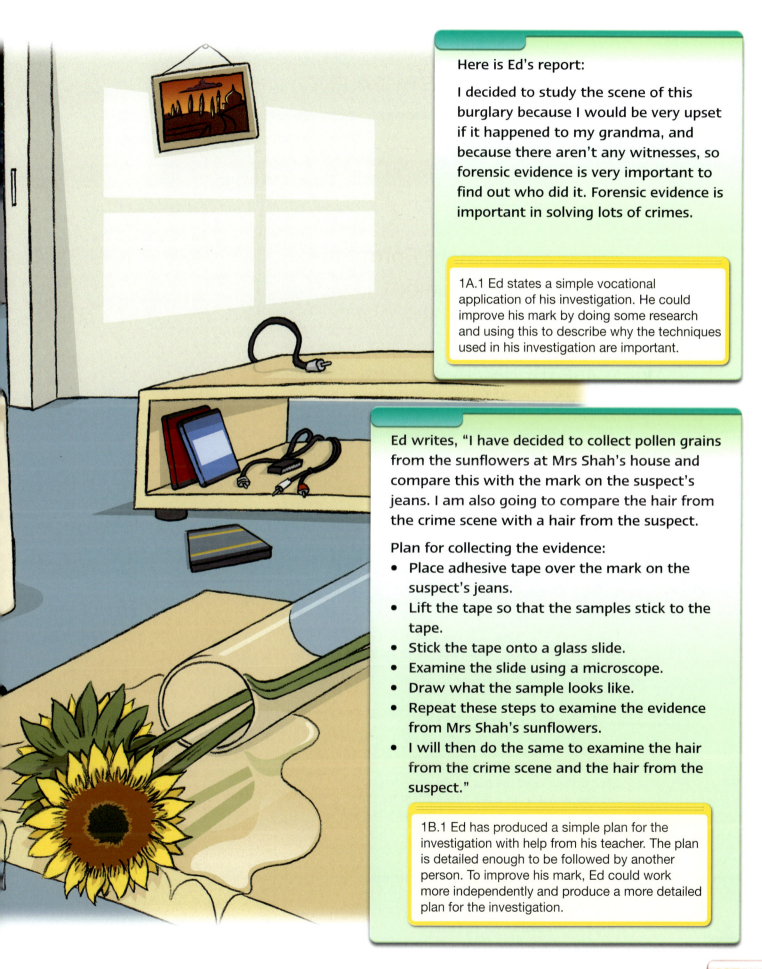

Here is Ed's report:

I decided to study the scene of this burglary because I would be very upset if it happened to my grandma, and because there aren't any witnesses, so forensic evidence is very important to find out who did it. Forensic evidence is important in solving lots of crimes.

1A.1 Ed states a simple vocational application of his investigation. He could improve his mark by doing some research and using this to describe why the techniques used in his investigation are important.

Ed writes, "I have decided to collect pollen grains from the sunflowers at Mrs Shah's house and compare this with the mark on the suspect's jeans. I am also going to compare the hair from the crime scene with a hair from the suspect.

Plan for collecting the evidence:
- Place adhesive tape over the mark on the suspect's jeans.
- Lift the tape so that the samples stick to the tape.
- Stick the tape onto a glass slide.
- Examine the slide using a microscope.
- Draw what the sample looks like.
- Repeat these steps to examine the evidence from Mrs Shah's sunflowers.
- I will then do the same to examine the hair from the crime scene and the hair from the suspect."

1B.1 Ed has produced a simple plan for the investigation with help from his teacher. The plan is detailed enough to be followed by another person. To improve his mark, Ed could work more independently and produce a more detailed plan for the investigation.

STUDENT'S COMMENTARY

I have filled in this risk assessment for my investigation.

Risk Assessment Form

WHAT IS YOUR INVESTIGATION?

To make and examine slides of hair samples, pollen samples and an unknown stain.

WHAT ARE THE HAZARDS?

The glass slides could break. The unknown stain could be a dangerous substance.

WHAT ARE THE RISKS?

There is a medium risk. I could cut myself on broken glass. There is a very low risk that the unknown stain could be dangerous.

HOW CAN THE RISK BE CONTROLLED?

If I break a slide, I won't pick it up with bare hands. I will use a dustpan and brush and I will put it in the broken glass bucket so no one else cuts themselves.

I will be wearing gloves in case the unknown stain is dangerous. This will also stop me contaminating the evidence.

2B.2 Ed has used the guidelines provided by his teacher to carry out a risk assessment for the investigation. He could improve his mark by carrying out the risk assessment independently.

The evidence

Pollen from the sunflowers that were disturbed in Mrs Shah's room	The unknown mark on the suspect's jeans

Hair from Mrs Shah's front room	**Hair from the suspect**
Short brown hair	Short brown hair

2C.1 Ed has selected the appropriate equipment for the investigation with a little guidance from his teacher and has used it correctly and safely to carry out the plan to collect and record data accurately. To improve his work, Ed could work more independently. He could also plan to repeat his measurements to make them more reliable.

What it means

The pollen sample from Mrs Shah's house matches the stain on the suspect's jeans. This shows me that the suspect has been near sunflowers and may have disturbed the vase of sunflowers in Mrs Shah's house. The hair from the crime scene appears to be the same as the suspect's hair, but most men have short brown hair so this isn't very convincing.

1D.1 Ed has used the information collected from his investigation to draw some simple conclusions. He could analyse his results in more detail.

How my investigation could be improved

I think this investigation could have been improved if I had more sources of evidence. I would like to go back and look for any fibres that were left at the crime scene and see if they match the clothes the suspect was wearing.

I think my findings show that the suspect might be involved but they do not prove he was involved. I would now send the hair samples to be tested for DNA. This could be used to prove whether the suspect was in Mrs Shah's house.

2E.1 Ed has evaluated his investigation and made a valid suggestion as to how to improve it.

2E.2 Ed has suggested how the findings from his investigation could be used in the context of the forensic investigation. Ed could improve his mark by evaluating his work more thoroughly:

- What were the strengths and weaknesses in his investigation?
- How could he collect more reliable and accurate evidence?

Break-in at the school canteen

Background

Mrs Webb had been a dinner lady at her local school for 15 years. Every morning she arrives at work at 6 o'clock to start cooking breakfasts for the children and staff before the start of the school day. But this morning was very different – as soon as she walked in, Mrs Webb realised something had happened. The skylights had been smashed and there were pieces of glass all over the floor. Then she noticed a half-eaten chocolate bar on the floor. Covering her hand with her jacket she opened the store cupboard door and saw that all the chocolate bars were gone. Mrs Webb closed the door carefully and used her mobile to phone the police. The police arrived and looked at the CCTV to identify two suspects, but the pictures were of poor quality and it was difficult to be sure they had identified the right people. The police would have to rely on forensic evidence to catch the people responsible. How could you find out who had broken into the school canteen?

Background

Dave enjoyed working at the garden centre and particularly liked looking after the plants and helping customers choose plants that would grow well in their gardens. When Dave arrived at work, his first job was to water the plants and check they were alright. As he went outside with his watering can he saw something was very wrong. Vandals must have broken into the garden centre the previous evening. Graffiti had been sprayed all over the walls and the empty can had been thrown on the floor. The pots of orange lilies, which had arrived the previous week, had been kicked around and the stems were broken and damaged. The police were called and they soon realised that this crime could be linked to two teenagers they had stopped the previous week for spraying paint over a park bench. How could you find out whether these boys were linked to damage at the garden centre?

What should I include?

To complete your investigation you need to:

- explain how your investigation can help to solve the crime
- produce a plan that is detailed enough for someone else to be able to follow
- carry out a risk assessment
- decide what equipment to use in your investigation
- carry out your plan carefully and collect and record your results
- process your results and explain your conclusions
- evaluate your investigation, explaining its strengths and weaknesses
- explain how your findings can be used as part of the police investigation

Unit summary

Concept map

The crime scene

Evidence is photographed before it is removed for analysis so that the crime scene can be reconstructed later.

Scene of Crime Officers search the crime scene for evidence.

Forensic scientists use the principle that every contact leaves a trace. Everyone who enters a crime scene will leave traces of evidence from themselves at the scene and pick up traces of evidence from the crime scene.

The crime scene is sealed off from the public to prevent evidence from being destroyed or contaminated.

Types of evidence

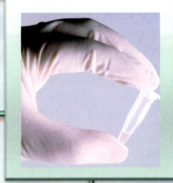

Typical samples taken from a crime scene include broken glass, fibres, fingerprints and blood.

Blood is often found at the scene of violent crimes such as murders, rapes or assaults. Blood group tests can be used to classify blood samples. Blood group tests are cheap and fast and can be carried out at the crime scene.

Fingerprints left at a crime scene or on items of evidence can be used to identify suspects, victims and witnesses.

DNA can be extracted from blood, semen or saliva samples. DNA profiling is used to identify suspects, witnesses and victims from evidence left at the crime scene.

Fibres are often found at crime scenes. They are easily transferred during struggles between people. Fibres are collected by placing adhesive tape onto the surface being tested and then carefully lifting the tape with the fibres now attached to it. The fibres can then be examined using a microscope.

Analysing evidence

Flame tests can be used to identify metals in compounds.

Some metal ions can be identified by observing their reaction with sodium hydroxide solution.

Samples that contain sulfate ions react with a solution of barium chloride to form a white precipitate.

Samples that contain carbonate ions react with acids to form the gas carbon dioxide, which turns limewater cloudy.

Samples that contain chloride ions react with acidified silver nitrate solution to form a white precipitate.

Unit quiz

1. Why do ionic compounds have high melting points?

2. How do we describe a substance that dissolves in water to form a solution?

3. What does TLC stand for?

4. Where in a cell is DNA found?

5. How can the refractive index of a glass block be calculated?

6. How is DNA analysed?

7. Name the **three** main types of fingerprint patterns.

8. What does SOCO stand for?

9. Name the **four** different blood group types.

10. How do we test for chloride ions?

11. What are the distinctive marks left on bullets when they are fired from a gun called?

12. What is the colour of the precipitate formed when sodium hydroxide solution is added to a solution that contains Cu^{2+} ions?

Numeracy activity

Blood groups

Around the world, different populations have different frequencies of blood groups. The table shows the frequency of different blood groups in the Netherlands.

Blood group	Percentage of population
O	?
A	43
B	9
AB	3

QUESTIONS

1. Complete the table by filling in the percentage of the Dutch population who have blood group O.

2. Draw a bar graph to show the information in the table.

3. Compare the number of people with blood group B and the number of people with blood group AB.

Exam practice

1 When a police officer arrives at a crime scene, their first duty is to help people.

a Why does the police officer then seal off the crime scene from the public? [1]

b If a suspect is identified, they can be removed from the scene. This stops the suspect from running away and allows the police to interview them. Give another reason why it is useful to remove the suspect from the crime scene. [1]

c Why do forensic scientists wear protective overalls when they examine a crime scene? [1]

d Why do forensic scientists limit the number of people who enter the crime scene? [1]

2 A photographer is a very important part of a forensic science team.

a Why are photographs taken before any evidence is removed from a crime scene? [1]

b The photographer will often place a ruler next to an item before photographing it. Why do they do this? [1]

3 Fingerprints are often left at crime scenes or on pieces of evidence. There are three types of fingerprint pattern. An example of each is shown below.

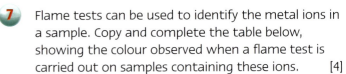

| A | B | C |

a Name the three types of fingerprint **A**, **B** and **C**. [3]

b Describe how a forensic scientist can reveal the fingerprints left at a crime scene. [1]

c Write down how fingerprints can be collected from a crime scene. [1]

d Why is a database of fingerprints very useful to the police? [1]

4 Forensic scientists use a wide range of techniques to try and work out what has happened at a crime scene. Suggest how a forensic scientist could solve the following problems. [6]

a Deciding whether two bullets have been fired by the same gun.

b Proving that two people are related to each other.

c Proving that a sample contains Fe(II) ions.

d Proving that the glass fragments found on a suspect's clothes match broken glass found at a crime scene.

e Proving that a sample of ink contains a mixture of different coloured inks.

f Finding out if a sample of water is neutral.

5 Identical twins are formed when a fertilised egg splits into two embryos.

a Why can't DNA evidence be used to differentiate between identical twins? [1]

b How can forensic scientists differentiate between identical twins? [1]

6 Fibres are long, thin, flexible materials. They are often found at crime scenes.

a How are fibres collected from a crime scene? [1]

b Explain how fibre evidence can be used to link a suspect to a crime scene. [1]

c Why do some types of fibre provide more convincing evidence of a link between a suspect and the crime scene than other types of fibre? [1]

7 Flame tests can be used to identify the metal ions in a sample. Copy and complete the table below, showing the colour observed when a flame test is carried out on samples containing these ions. [4]

Metal ions in the sample	Colour of flame test
Potassium	
Calcium	
Sodium	
Copper	

(Total 27 marks)

Worked example

Broken glass is often found at crime scenes.
When glass breaks, tiny pieces scatter over a large area.

We measure the amount a sample of glass refracts
light by calculating the refractive index of the material.
Different types of glass refract light by slightly different
amounts and have slightly different refractive indexes.

a Measure angle x.   [1]

b Measure angle y.   [1]

c What is the name given to angle x?   [1]

d What is the name given to angle y?   [1]

e Calculate the refractive index of the glass block.   [3]

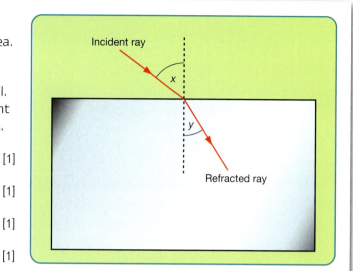

This is the correct answer. Remember to take a protractor to measure these angles accurately.

This is the correct answer. Remember to measure the angle between the ray and normal.

This is the correct answer. Take care to make sure you get these the right way round.

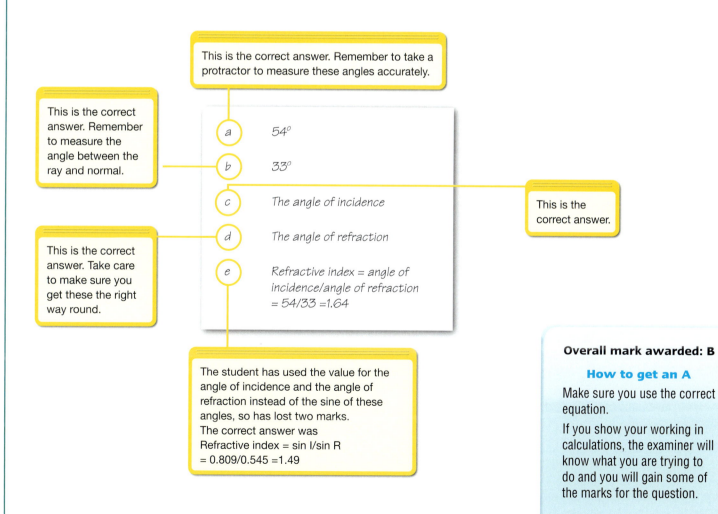

a 54°

b 33°

c The angle of incidence

d The angle of refraction

e Refractive index = angle of incidence/angle of refraction
= 54/33 =1.64

This is the correct answer.

The student has used the value for the angle of incidence and the angle of refraction instead of the sine of these angles, so has lost two marks.
The correct answer was
Refractive index = sin I/sin R
= 0.809/0.545 =1.49

Overall mark awarded: B

How to get an A
Make sure you use the correct equation.

If you show your working in calculations, the examiner will know what you are trying to do and you will gain some of the marks for the question.

Sports science

DISCOVER ATHLETICS!

Building muscles and using energy requires very good nutrition. If an athlete's diet is not perfect for their needs, they will never become world champion.

Athletes push themselves to the limit. Training programmes have to be designed to develop maximum strength in muscles, and maximum fitness and stamina without causing injury.

Every athlete dreams of being the best in the world. But however talented they are, no athlete can become an Olympic champion on their own. They are supported by teams of people who are specialists in nutrition, in how the human body works, in developing and monitoring training programmes and in designing equipment. Sport and science are very closely linked.

Good quality equipment is essential. Poor quality equipment is much harder to use and increases the athlete's risk of strain or injury. New materials mean the quality of sports equipment is improving all the time.

Success in sport

You will find out:

- What factors affect a person's success in sport
- How some of these factors improve performance in sport

Win or lose?

Did you always win all the running games at primary school? Or were you always last to be picked for the teams? Most of us are somewhere between the two – we're fairly good at some sports but we'll never win anything! So what is it that makes some people really good at sports, and is there anything that the rest of us can do to improve?

Being prepared

You know that to do well in your GCSE science you have to do some learning first, then some revision. **Athletes** work in the same way; they learn the best type of **training** to do, then keep practising. Our **muscles** get stronger if we use them regularly, and so do our **heart** and **lungs**, so someone who doesn't do much physical **exercise** will always get fitter if they start exercising regularly. But it is important to start gently; exercising too hard using muscles that are not used to it can cause injury. In older people it can even cause heart attacks, because the heart suddenly has to do more work than it can cope with. The right food is important too; your body cannot work at its best without enough **energy** and **nutrients**. Athletes are very careful about what they eat and when.

Being competitive

All the best athletes are very **competitive**; they really want to win. For many top-class athletes, their training is the most important thing in their life. They watch what they eat carefully, even on holiday, avoiding all the foods that are nice but not good for them. They concentrate hard on their training, even when they don't want to, and can stay focused on winning even when surrounded by distractions such as bad weather, feeling tired, or noisy crowds. They just seem to be able to 'push themselves' that bit harder than most of us.

FIGURE 1: Are these future champions? How could you tell?

FIGURE 2: How do you decide which are the right foods to eat?

FIGURE 3: Athletes have to be prepared to train all year round, whatever the weather.

QUESTIONS

1. Why does someone get fitter if they start exercising regularly?
2. State **two** problems that can be caused by exercising too hard if you are not used to it.
3. Describe what we mean when we say an athlete is 'competitive'.
4. Give **two** examples of things that athletes do to help them win.

...athletes ...competitive ...energy ...exercise ...fit ...healthy

Being fit

Are you **fit**? Being fit means different things for different people. A toddler can be fit, so can a teenager, so can a retired person, but you would not expect all these people to do the same things. Being fit means having a **healthy** body with all its systems working well, ready to meet whatever demands you make of it. What a fit person can do changes as they get older; that's why athletes often retire in their thirties. They are still very fit, but their bodies are no longer able to do as much as a younger athlete can, so they can no longer win competitions. To keep fit, you must exercise, but you must also eat the right combination of nutrients to maintain muscle development and supply energy. This 'right combination of nutrients' depends on the type of sport you do.

Being equipped

In May 1954, Roger Bannister became the first athlete in the world to run a mile in under four minutes. Now all really good long-distance runners can complete a 'four minute mile'. Most other sporting records are the same; world records keep getting beaten by faster times, longer distances and so on. If you have ever held an old tennis or badminton racquet, you will have noticed they are very heavy compared with the racquets we use today. Bikes and boats were heavier, cricket bats broke more easily, crash mats didn't exist. Modern athletes train better and use much better clothing and equipment than athletes used to, and that's due to the work of **sports scientists**.

FIGURE 4: Many things have changed in sports since 1954 when Roger Bannister first ran a mile in four minutes.

WOW FACTOR!

Experts say we need to exercise for 20 minutes, three times a week, to stay reasonably fit.

Made to run?

In 2003, Australian sports scientists announced that they had found a gene that is linked to athletic performance. The gene has two variants: one (that they called the 'sprint' variant) is more common in sprinters and one (that they called the 'endurance' variant) is more common in long-distance runners. They showed that the sprint variant of the gene produces a protein found in muscles used for running fast, and so makes people more likely to excel at sprinting events.

	sprinters	endurance runners	general population
'sprint' variant	50%	31%	30%
'endurance' variant	5%	24%	18%
mixture	45%	45%	52%

TABLE 1: Prevalence of the 'sprint' gene and the 'endurance' gene in sprinters, endurance runners and the general population.

WANT TO KNOW MORE?

Doctors link several health problems to an inactive lifestyle. Can you find out what some of these problems are?

QUESTIONS

5   List **four** things that success in sport depends on.

6   Discuss what you would mean by 'fit' for an 'ordinary' person and for an athlete.

7   Choose **one** sport. Do some research to find out how the equipment used has changed.

QUESTIONS

8   "If you have the 'endurance' variant of the gene you are likely to become a good long-distance runner." Discuss to what extent the figures in the table show this statement to be either right or wrong.

Sports scientists

You will find out:
- Some of the areas a sports scientist might work in
- What skills sports scientists need to use, and the challenges they face

Going to the gym

Every January, the number of people taking out membership at a gym suddenly increases. Many people realise that they have eaten too much over Christmas, or they are not as fit as they would like to be. Going to the gym certainly helps, but it doesn't make them all into top-class athletes! There's more to it than just making an effort – but what?

FIGURE 1: What are the benefits of going to a gym?

What do sports scientists do?

The job of a **sports scientist** is to help athletes improve their **performance** in competitions. Success in sport depends on lots of things, such as the **health** and **nutrition** of the athlete, how effective their **training** programme is and what **equipment** they are using, so sports scientists are involved in all of these areas. Sport physiologists help athletes to monitor and improve their general health and **fitness**. Sports **dieticians** monitor nutrition and help develop diets that are perfect for a particular athlete's needs. **Materials scientists** design and develop sports equipment that is effective and is easy and comfortable to use. If they are to do their best, athletes need all of these people.

Using scientific methods

A good scientist needs to be able to make accurate observations, decide what he or she needs to find out more about, make suitable measurements to collect the necessary data and then use that data to increase his or her knowledge and understanding. Sports scientists are no different. Their work includes various ways of monitoring the performance of athletes and the changes that happen in an athlete's body during exercise. They might also be involved in testing the strength, or other properties, of materials used to make sporting equipment. And, of course, they have to be able to decide suitable ways to share what they find with athletes and other scientists.

FIGURE 2: How might a personal trainer help an athlete improve?

QUESTIONS

1. Describe in your own words what the job of a sports scientist is.
2. Describe **two** things that sports scientists may be involved in.
3. Describe **two** things that a sports scientist needs to be able to do.
4. Discuss some of the things that a sports scientist might monitor. Make a list.

...calories   ...dieticians   ...equipment   ...fitness   ...health

Developing fitness

Athletes push themselves very hard. They always have a very high level of overall fitness, but athletes in different sports need bodies that can perform in different ways. For example, a sprinter's body needs to be able to supply an enormous amount of energy for a very short time, but a marathon runner will need stamina to run at a slower speed for a very long time. It is the job of sports scientists to design training programmes that meet these different needs.

Changing diets

Everybody needs more **calories** if they do more exercise and use more energy, but athletes need much more than just a diet high in calories. Sports dieticians have to design different diets for different types of athletes, and for different times in their training programmes, with exactly the right foods to build muscles, or to supply energy, or to replace fluids and minerals lost during competition. Also, if possible, the diet has to take account of an individual's likes and dislikes, or they may not stick to it!

Designing equipment

New materials are being developed all the time. It is the job of materials scientists working in sport to assess the properties of new materials and to decide if or how they can be used in sporting equipment. For example, a change in the material used for trainer soles might reduce leg injuries in runners, or a change in the elasticity (bounciness) of a racquet might enable an athlete to hit a ball further or faster. But the scientists must also ensure that the improvement in one property, such as elasticity, does not cause a problem by affecting a different property, such as strength.

FIGURE 3: Tennis doesn't look like this any more! Discuss the advantages of modern style racquets compared with this wooden one.

What are the limits?

Veterinary scientists and trainers put as much effort into trying to improve the performance of racehorses as is spent helping human athletes improve. Yet the top speed of the fastest racehorses has hardly changed in hundreds of years. It has been suggested that perhaps racehorses have reached a natural limit, because the bones in their legs are not strong enough to cope with the physical stresses that would be caused by galloping faster.

FIGURE 4: Is there a limit to how fast racehorses can gallop?

QUESTIONS

7 Find out how the sporting records for a sport of your choice have changed over time. Can you suggest reasons for the changes? Is there any evidence for 'natural limits' in your chosen sport?

QUESTIONS

5 Choose **two** athletes from different sports not mentioned in the text. Discuss how their fitness might differ.

6 Work together to list the basic types of nutrients in a balanced diet, and say what they are needed for.

The body at rest

You will find out:
- How the human cardiovascular system works
- What lung capacity and tidal volume are, and how to measure them

How fit are you?

You perhaps judge how fit you are by how much sport you do. Any kind of physical activity, such as skateboarding or even walking your dog, will make you fitter. But activity that is too sudden or too strenuous can cause injury, so it is important to be able to assess someone's fitness before they start exercising, not just afterwards. To do that, you need to know how the body works.

FIGURE 1: Will skateboarding make you fit?

The heart of the matter

The heart, lungs and blood vessels in your body all work together to get oxygen from the air into all the cells in your body, where it is needed. They form the **cardiovascular system**. The right-hand side of your heart pumps blood to your lungs, where the blood passes around very thin-walled air sacs called **alveoli**. Carbon dioxide from the blood passes into the alveoli, and oxygen from air in the alveoli passes into the blood. The blood returns to the left-hand side of your heart, which pumps it around to the rest of your body. In your cells, the oxygen is used for **respiration**, and waste carbon dioxide from respiration is absorbed into the blood, to be carried back to your heart, then to your lungs and so on.

Your pulse is a measure of your heart rate. The average resting pulse of healthy adults is about 70 beats a minute, though it is generally faster in younger people and slower in fitter people.

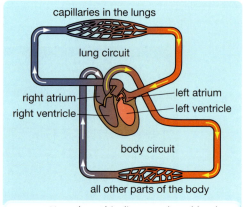

capillaries in the lungs

lung circuit

right atrium
right ventricle

left atrium
left ventricle

body circuit

all other parts of the body

FIGURE 2: How does this diagram show blood containing lots of oxygen?

Take a deep breath

Figure 3 shows how we can model what happens when we breathe in and out. When we breathe in, muscles move our ribs upwards and outwards, and pull our diaphragm downwards. This makes the lungs fill with air, just as the balloons in the model fill with air if you pull the rubber sheet downwards. When you breathe out, muscles relax, your ribs move downwards and inwards, your diaphragm curves upwards, and air is pushed out of your lungs.

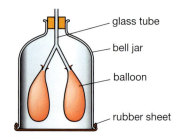

glass tube

bell jar

balloon

rubber sheet

FIGURE 3: How is the bell jar experiment similar to and different from real breathing?

QUESTIONS

1 Which organs make up the cardiovascular system?
2 Where is the blood from each side of your heart pumped to?
3 Discuss how someone's resting pulse rate could help you tell how fit they are. What else would you need to know about them?

...alveoli ...cardiovascular system ...haemoglobin ...lung capacity

Lung capacity and tidal volume

Some people just seem to have a lot more 'puff' than others – but the size of someone's **thorax** (their chest) is not often a good guide to how much 'puff' they have. That is because the amount of 'puff' we have is usually a measure of how efficiently we use our lungs, not of how big they are. Athletes train to use their lungs as efficiently as possible.

A **spirometer** measures **lung capacity** and **tidal volume**. Figure 4 shows a simple, but less accurate, way of measuring these. Our lung capacity is a measure of how much air our lungs can hold; to measure it, you take a deep breath and measure the maximum amount of air you breathe out (the water you can displace by blowing into the bottle). The tidal volume of our lungs is the amount of air that we breathe out when we are breathing normally. Athletes have a larger lung capacity, and a larger tidal volume, than non-athletes.

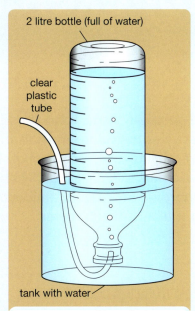

2 litre bottle (full of water)

clear plastic tube

tank with water

FIGURE 4: How could you find out how much air is left in your lungs after you have breathed out?

Carrying oxygen

In the lungs, the air spreads out into about 300 million alveoli, having a total surface area of about 70 m^2. These alveoli are surrounded by tiny blood vessels called capillaries, making the flow of oxygen and carbon dioxide between the alveoli and the blood very efficient. The oxygen binds chemically to a protein called **haemoglobin** in the red blood cells. A healthy diet, rich in iron, helps the formation of haemoglobin and so enables the blood to carry more oxygen. Some toxic chemicals, such as carbon monoxide, bind to the haemoglobin instead of oxygen, so cells do not have the oxygen they need for respiration.

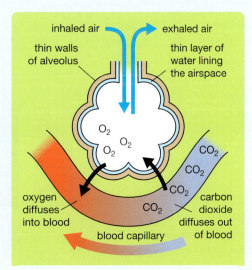

inhaled air   exhaled air

thin walls of alveolus

thin layer of water lining the airspace

O_2 O_2 O_2

CO_2 CO_2 CO_2 CO_2

oxygen diffuses into blood

carbon dioxide diffuses out of blood

blood capillary

FIGURE 5: In some diseases, the surface area of the alveoli decreases. What symptom might this cause?

William Harvey

Until the 1600s, scientists believed the blood in veins and arteries was quite separate. The blood in veins was made in the liver, then pumped into the body by the heart to nourish it. The blood in arteries contained air from the lungs to cool the heart down. In the early 1600s, William Harvey calculated that the heart pumped about 3.6 litres of blood in a minute – that's over 5 tonnes of blood in a day! So Harvey realised that the blood in the veins and arteries must be the same small amount of blood circulating around, and worked out how the cardiovascular system works.

QUESTIONS

4   Describe the difference between lung capacity and tidal volume.

5   Explain the importance of the alveoli in breathing.

6   Children with asthma or other illnesses that cause breathing problems are sometimes advised to learn a wind instrument. Discuss how this might help them.

QUESTIONS

7   More recent medical developments include designing fluids that can be breathed instead of air. Find out about these and where they are useful.

Adapted for exercise

You will find out:

- How antagonistic pairs of muscles work
- What changes happen in the body during exercise
- The difference between aerobic and anaerobic respiration

Active is best!

People who are physically active are generally fitter than those who aren't, but does it matter? Many scientific studies have shown that an inactive lifestyle is a major risk factor for several illnesses, such as high blood pressure, heart disease and even Alzheimer's disease. Studies have also shown that physical activity helps improve our mental abilities, such as memory and learning, and can even make us feel happier.

Muscles

The human body contains nearly 650 named **muscles**, and thousands of unnamed ones. Without them we could not move, or breathe, or see clearly, or digest our food. All muscles contain special cells that can contract (get shorter), and then relax again. Muscles cannot push – they can only **contract** and pull. When muscles 'push' blood out of our heart, or food through our digestive system, what is really happening is that a ring of muscles is contracting. This makes the ring smaller and squeezes the blood or the food out. Our heart muscles are very strong; they contract and relax the heart about once a second, day and night, every day of our lives. Try clenching your fist, then relaxing, once a second, and see how long it is before your hand gets tired! You can test the strength of your muscles in your hands by gripping or squeezing bathroom scales and measuring the reading they give. The harder you can squeeze, the stronger your muscles are.

Antagonistic pairs

Because muscles can only pull, there are many places in our bodies where we need two muscles – one to bend our arm, for example, and one to straighten it out again. Figure 3 shows the main muscles in the upper arm. To flex (bend) your arm, the biceps muscle contracts, and the triceps muscle relaxes. To extend (straighten) your arm again, the biceps muscle relaxes and the triceps muscle contracts. Muscles working like this are called an **antagonistic pair**.

FIGURE 1: What are the benefits of an active lifestyle?

FIGURE 2: Muscles in our face help us express our feelings. Can you feel where any of the muscles in your face are?

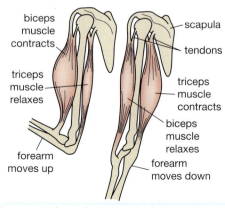

biceps muscle contracts

scapula

tendons

triceps muscle relaxes

triceps muscle contracts

biceps muscle relaxes

forearm moves up

forearm moves down

FIGURE 3: Where else in your body do you have pairs of muscles like this?

▌ QUESTIONS ▐

1 List **four** things we could not do without muscles.

2 Describe in your own words how muscles 'push' blood out of our heart.

3 Work with a partner to identify at least **three** other places in our bodies where we have antagonistic pairs of muscles.

...*aerobic* ...*anaerobic* ...*antagonistic pair* ...*contract*

The changes during exercise

Muscles use energy when they contract. The muscle cells get their energy from **respiration** within the cells. Glucose and oxygen, carried to the cells in the blood, are changed into energy, water and waste carbon dioxide. The more work our muscles do, the more oxygen they need, and the more waste carbon dioxide they produce. So, as we exercise, our pulse rate goes up as our heart beats faster to increase the amount of blood going to the cells. We breathe faster and deeper as our lungs supply the extra oxygen needed.

Aerobic or anaerobic?

Normally the respiration in our muscle cells is **aerobic** – it uses oxygen. The equation for aerobic respiration is:

FIGURE 4: Why do athletes need to rest after exercising hard?

glucose + oxygen → carbon dioxide + water + energy

$$C_6H_{12}O_6 + 6O_2 \rightarrow 6CO_2 + 6H_2O + 2900 \text{ kJ}$$

If we exercise very hard or for a very long time, our lungs cannot work hard enough to supply all the oxygen needed. We say our muscles have an **oxygen debt**. Our muscles begin to break down glucose without using oxygen. This is called **anaerobic** respiration and the equation is:

glucose → lactic acid + energy

$$C_6H_{12}O_6 \rightarrow 2C_3H_6O_3 + 120 \text{ kJ}$$

You can see that anaerobic respiration is not as efficient as aerobic respiration. It only supplies 120 kJ of energy from each molecule of glucose, not 2900 kJ.

Lactic acid is toxic to cells, so when it builds in muscles it makes them ache, and may cause cramps. After exercise, you continue to breathe heavily until the extra oxygen this supplies has broken down all the lactic acid into carbon dioxide and water. Your **recovery rate** is the time it takes for heart rate and breathing to return to normal. Athletes recover more quickly than non-athletes because their breathing is more efficient and supplies more oxygen.

WOW FACTOR!

Scientists have found that astronauts lose up to 10% of their heart muscle after only a few days of physical inactivity in space.

QUESTIONS

4 Give **two** changes that happen when we exercise. Explain why they happen.

5 Describe the difference between aerobic and anaerobic respiration.

6 Write a word equation for the breakdown of lactic acid. Work together to write a balanced symbol equation for the process.

EXAM HINTS AND TIPS

Remember: Muscles cannot push, they can only contract and pull.

Aerobic exercise

FIGURE 5: How fast should your heart beat during exercise?

The body works most efficiently during aerobic exercise. Regular aerobic exercise causes muscles to grow in size and strength to cope with the additional demands. Anaerobic exercise can delay muscle development by breaking down muscle tissue to supply the energy needed immediately. Scientists have calculated the minimum and maximum heart rates for efficient aerobic exercise. They are 65% and 85% of (220 – athlete's age in years). Less fit people should start exercising at the minimum heart rate, and only increase heart rate gradually. Only highly trained athletes, under appropriate supervision, should exercise at above the maximum heart rate.

QUESTIONS

7 Find out more about the training programmes recommended to help unfit people, or those recovering from illness, return to fitness.

All under control

You will find out:
- The effects of exercise on your body
- How your body controls temperature, water and glucose levels

Diabetes and exercise

The woman in figure 1 has diabetes, a disease where the body does not control the levels of glucose in the blood properly. She is injecting insulin, one of the hormones that control the amount of glucose in the blood. Athletes with diabetes compete successfully in many different sports, but they have to monitor their blood, and control their diet and their medication, very carefully before and during exercise, because physical activity can use up glucose very rapidly.

FIGURE 1: Do you know the warning signs to watch for if someone you know has diabetes?

How does it feel?

Exercising hard doesn't just make you breathe faster and make your heart beat faster. It also leaves you sweaty, flushed and thirsty. These changes keep the conditions in your body just right for your cells to work well. If the **temperature** in your body is too high or too low, or if there is too much or too little **water**, or too much or too little **glucose**, the cells stop working properly. If the problem is not solved, you become ill and eventually die.

Cooling down

When you exercise, some of the **energy** produced by **respiration** in your muscle cells is used to make your muscles contract. A lot of energy is lost as wasted heat energy, carried away from the cells in your blood. You look red after exercise because blood **capillaries** just under your skin dilate (get wider) to allow more blood to flow close to the surface of your body to be cooled by the air outside. If this does not cool you enough, you start sweating. The **sweat** evaporates from your skin to help cool you down.

FIGURE 2: Describe all the changes you notice when you exercise.

Feeling thirsty

Your body is about two-thirds water. As you sweat, you lose water. Your body tries to save water by producing less, more concentrated, **urine**. If you lose too much water you will become dehydrated, causing tiredness, poor concentration, headaches and forgetfulness. Losing 3% of your body's water can cause serious problems; losing 10% is fatal. Athletes drink during training and competition to replace the water they lose.

FIGURE 3: Do you know how much water you should drink each day?

▌▌ QUESTIONS ▐▐

1. List **five** effects on your body of exercising hard.
2. Describe **two** ways your body uses to cool down.
3. How does your body try to save water when you lose water by sweating?
4. Suggest some sports where it would be very important to drink during competition.

...capillaries ...energy ...glucagon ...glucose ...glycogen ...insulin

Controlling glucose

All the cells in your body need a steady supply of glucose to make the energy they need. The glucose comes from the food you eat, so there is a lot available when you've just eaten a meal, and not enough if you haven't eaten for a while. When there is plenty of glucose available, your body stores the excess glucose in the liver, and in long-chain molecules called **glycogen** in your muscles. The glycogen molecules are a way of storing the glucose for later, because your cells can't use the glycogen for respiration. When there is no longer enough glucose available, some of the stored glucose is released into your blood. This keeps the level of glucose in your blood, and thus going to your cells, almost constant.

Insulin and glucagon

Two hormones, **insulin** and **glucagon**, control the storage and release of glucose. Just after a meal, the high levels of glucose cause cells called beta cells in the **pancreas** to release insulin into the blood. The insulin makes the liver absorb glucose, and other cells combine glucose molecules together to form long glycogen molecules. When the level of glucose in the blood falls too low, the release of insulin stops and cells in the pancreas called alpha cells release glucagon. The glucagon stimulates the liver to release glucose and the other cells to break down glycogen into glucose again, so it can be used for respiration.

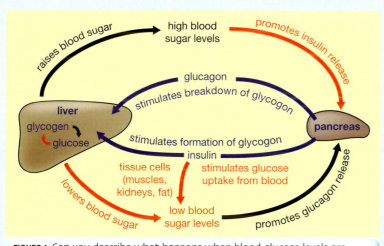

FIGURE 4: Can you describe what happens when blood glucose levels are high?

Too much water?

Athletes are often told 'drink plenty of fluids', but drinking too much can cause coma or even death. Usually the amount of water in the blood is controlled by the kidneys, but if fears of dehydration cause an athlete to drink too much water in a short time, the concentration of salts in their blood is diluted. At the same time salts are being lost in sweat, so the concentration of salts can fall dangerously low, causing the brain, heart and muscles to stop functioning properly. The simplest advice to athletes to prevent this is 'only drink if you feel thirsty'.

QUESTIONS

5   Describe when insulin is released into the blood and why.

6   What level of glycogen would you expect an athlete to have in their muscles at the end of a marathon, and why?

7   Discuss the benefits of sugary snacks and carbohydrate snacks during activity.

QUESTIONS

8   One way athletes test whether or not they tend to drink too much during training or competition is to weigh themselves before and after. Suggest how this might help.

Keep running

INVESTIGATION

In this investigation, Will and his group are designing a personal fitness plan for a cross-country runner. Will is going to try this plan out on himself so that the group can monitor its effectiveness.

Will writes: "The purpose of the plan is to build up my stamina and to reduce the time it takes me to run a typical course. This will be done by developing my muscles and my lung capacity and by enabling my blood to carry more oxygen around my body. In cross-country running it is stamina that is important. There isn't any quick way of improving; it's a case of developing a strategy and sticking to it over a period of time."

2A.1 Will has described a vocational application of this investigation and has clearly shown how it relates to his chosen area of sport. To develop the work further, he could incorporate more scientific ideas when explaining how his personal fitness plan is going to work.

Here is Will's plan:

The first part of the plan was to establish current fitness levels. I did this by means of a beep test, which is the usual way of doing it. You run from one line to another in the gym. When the beep sounds, you have to have reached the second of two lines or you are eliminated. When you hear it, you run back to the first line, and so on. The beeps are pre-recorded and the interval between them gets less and less. I got to Level 15, which is pretty good.

I also had to allow for injuries (mildly strained ankles at the end of the previous season) and health problems (none); and then to build in physical activities in a typical week. In my case, this was two four-hour surfing sessions a week in the summer and two two-hour running sessions a week in the winter. I could then set a target, which was to complete the 4200 m practice course in 14 minutes. My fastest time before that was 14 minutes 24 seconds.

Safety is very important, as you have to avoid injury in order to be fit and be selected for teams. The main thing is to build up to the hardest part of a training session and wind down afterwards. The warm-up and warm-down sessions are very important.

In order to make sure that the tasks lead to meeting targets, the sessions have to have the correct structure. You get to be a better runner by running, but just doing more running simply tires you out. Therefore, different sessions are structured in different ways. In my plan we have organised three sessions each week for five weeks.

In the first session each week, I will run a succession of 1000 m distances. In the second I will do a 'fartlek', which is a mixed pace session. The first part is typically walked, the next part jogged, the next run and the final part sprinted. The third session is a run of a race session distance.

As the weeks go by, so the activities will be changed, principally with the fartlek sessions, in which the distances walked and jogged will be reduced and the amounts run and sprinted will be increased. The plan had to be submitted to the teacher.

3B.1 Will has developed a clear and well structured plan. Each part is justified, with an explanation of why it is there, and the plan is detailed enough for someone else to see the structure clearly. Will could develop the plan further by explaining more about the effects of the different parts of the plan on the development of running ability and include more detail about how the plan might be modified during the six weeks.

STUDENT'S COMMENTARY

Will also had to complete a risk assessment form.

Risk Assessment Form

DESCRIBE THE INVESTIGATION

I am going to be doing a lot of running in my investigation. Some of it will be indoors and some outdoors. Running can be dangerous, so I will need to work safely.

WHAT ARE THE HAZARDS?

The main hazard is that when you are running you might trip and fall. There is also a hazard because if you are running with other people and you are all wearing running shoes, you might get spiked by one of the other runners. You might pull a muscle if you start running too fast, too soon.

WHAT ARE THE RISKS?

You might get injured from a fall, or you might get cut from another runner's spikes, or you might get a pulled muscle.

HOW CAN THE RISK BE CONTROLLED?

You have to be careful when you are running, especially if the floor is very smooth if you are indoors or slippery if you are outside. You mustn't get too close to other runners if you are wearing spikes, and also you have to be careful to warm up at the start of exercise and warm down at the end.

WHAT IS THE REMAINING RISK?

You can never be 100% sure that you won't get hurt, because running is a physical activity, but I think that if I do all of these things I am very likely to complete my investigation without being injured.

2B.2 Will completed a risk assessment, although the structure gave him a certain amount of support. It was appropriate but he could have scored a higher mark if he had planned it himself.

What I found out

As the third training session each week was to run a race-length course, it was easy to monitor progress towards the target over the six weeks that the plan was tested over. My PB (personal best) on the race-length course (in the school grounds) was 14 minutes 24 seconds, so each week I could see how I was doing.

Week	Race length course time	Notes
1	14 m 32s	First week back after half term; not yet fully fit
2	14 m 26 s	Good run, ideal conditions
3	14 m 21 s	Really good run
4	14 m 28 s	Harsh wind blowing
5	14 m 9 s	Clear day, cold but ideal conditions
6	14 m 11 s	Bit drizzly but ground firm

> 2C.1 Will has gathered appropriate data and displayed it in an effective way. He has made accurate timings over the same set distance at weekly intervals and made notes about the prevalent conditions. Repeat readings would not be appropriate in this context, but he might look to gathering data from other parts of the running activities to support this set.

What the experiment shows

The experiment shows three things. Firstly it shows that my times tended to improve over the six weeks. Three of the runs were less than my previous PB. Secondly it shows that I didn't reach the target of 14 minutes. This was disappointing, but perhaps the target was a bit unrealistic. I do quite a lot of physical activity already, including a lot of running, so trying to knock 24 seconds off my PB in six weeks was a lot to ask.

Thirdly it showed how the conditions affect the times. None of the days were really slippery, but on two of them the weather was quite bad and that makes a difference. Also, none of these were in competitive situations, and it's this that gives the best times in my experience.

> 1E.1 Will has included a simple evaluation of the effectiveness of the investigation, identifying other factors that affect performance. He needs to suggest what an improved investigation might involve.

A sports scientist might be able to make use of this data to design a personal fitness plan for other people. It shows how you start from current fitness levels, amounts of activity and health record. It also shows how working towards a target is not always a gradual process, and it shows how you have to match the activities to the target, otherwise you might be active but not getting any faster.

> 2D.1 Will has examined the data carefully to identify the underlying pattern and to draw conclusions that are appropriate. He has been limited by the range of data gathered as to how firm his conclusions could be.

> 2E.2 Will has suggested how a sports scientist might make use of such a plan and also what limitations might have to accepted with this.

Energy for living

You will find out:

● Why eating a balanced diet is important

● What body mass index is and how to calculate it

● How to calculate a person's basic energy requirement

Eating well?

A health survey published in 2004 suggested that nearly half of teenage girls in Britain and over a third of teenage boys are overweight or obese. Another survey said that almost three-quarters of parents thought that their teenagers did not do enough exercise at school. But why do doctors and parents worry about teenagers' weight or exercise? Does it matter?

A balanced diet

You have already learnt about the importance of a balanced diet in the Food science unit, but it is important to revise it here because exercise is not enough to keep you healthy if you do not eat a balanced diet. It must include foods that provide protein, carbohydrates, fats and oils, vitamins and minerals, and fibre. Dieticians recommend that we should eat at least five portions of fruit and vegetables each day (a portion is about a handful), but many of us don't. If your diet is mostly 'convenience foods', you are almost certainly eating more sugar and salt than you should. Doctors have shown that eating a poor diet, which is not balanced, increases our risk of heart disease, strokes, diabetes, cancer and many other diseases.

FIGURE 1: Discuss this meal. What is good, or bad, about it?

FIGURE 2: Do you eat enough fruit and vegetables?

How much food?

The energy in foods is measured in **kilocalories** (kcal) or **kilojoules** (kJ). Starchy, fatty and sweet foods contain many more kilocalories per 100 g than fruit or vegetables. Table 1 shows roughly the number of kilocalories needed by different people, but this is

Age (in years)	Daily calorie requirement (kcal)	
	Male	**Female**
1	1100	1100
7–10	2000	2000
11–14	2220	1845
15–18	2755	2110
Adult (sedentary)	2500	1900
Adult (active)	2700	2000

TABLE 1: How could you calculate approximately how many kilocalories you eat each day?

only a rough guide. The actual amount of energy you need each day depends on your height and weight (whether you are a stocky build or a very slim build), whether or not you are growing and how active you are. One of the reasons 'junk foods' are bad for us is that they give us the energy we need without giving us the necessary vitamins, minerals and fibre as well.

QUESTIONS

1 List the things that foods in a balanced diet should provide.

2 List some illnesses we are more likely to suffer from if we eat a poor diet.

3 Give **four** examples of foods that contain lots of energy and **four** that contain little.

4 Work with a partner to remember why we need each of the nutrients in a balanced diet.

Body mass index

Doctors use **body mass index** (**BMI**) to decide if a person is the weight they should be. It is a very useful measure because it can be used with both men and women of all ages, and with children. A person's BMI is calculated using the formula:

Body mass index (BMI) = weight (in kg) ÷ height² (in m²)

The table shows how BMI is related to ideal weight.

BMI	
Less than 18.5	Underweight
18.5 to 24.9	Normal weight
25.0 to 29.9	Overweight
30.0 to 39.9	Obese
40.0 or more	Extremely obese

FIGURE 3: What are the health risks of being obese?

There is a range of BMI values that are 'normal' because people have a range of body types – some large-boned or stocky, some very slim.

BMI can be used to find out approximately what weight a person should be. For example, a large-boned man 1.78 m tall should weigh approximately 79 kg. His BMI will be at the top end of the 'normal' range. So:

$$24.9 = \text{weight} \div (1.78)^2$$

$$\text{weight} = 24.9 \times (1.78)^2 = 79 \text{ kg}$$

Basic energy requirement

Your body needs energy for the basic life processes that keep you alive, such as breathing, staying warm, and repairing or replacing damaged cells. The amount of energy you need when you are inactive or resting is called your **basic energy requirement (BER)**. It depends on your weight, because a heavier person has more tissue that needs to be supplied with blood and oxygen and maintained at the correct temperature. You can calculate BER each hour using the formula:

basic energy requirement per hour (in kcal) = weight (in kg) × 1.3

So an inactive man whose weight is 70 kg would need 70 × 1.3 = 91 kcal per hour, or 70 × 1.3 × 24 = 2184 kcal per day.

If someone is dieting, they should calculate their BER using their ideal weight, not the weight they are.

Watch Out Weight is used in its everyday meaning here. The 'weight (in kg)' used here is actually mass. The unit of true weight is the Newton.

Body fat

Accurate machines to measure body fat use lasers to scan the body, using the reflected light to accurately plot body shape. At the same time, radio waves are passed through the body. How easily they are conducted through the body depends on whether they pass through fat or through other tissue. A computer then calculates the percentage of body fat. Healthy males should have approximately 15% body fat, while for women it should be approximately 20%. The exact value varies according to ethnic origin.

QUESTIONS

5 Why is there a range of values of body mass index for 'normal' weight?

6 Describe why you need energy even when you are inactive.

7 Calculate the body mass index and basic energy requirement per day for an inactive woman 1.60 m tall and weighing 55 kg.

QUESTIONS

8 Suggest why an athlete might be interested in measuring how their body fat percentage changes as well as how their weight changes.

The right diet

You will find out:
- Why a balanced diet is important
- How an athlete's diet varies from a 'normal' balanced diet
- How athletes monitor their diet

Malnutrition

The child in figure 1 shows what most of us think malnourished children look like. However, doctors are worried that there are growing numbers of children suffering malnutrition in wealthy countries. Some are eating 'junk' food, which contains the calories they need but without the right nutrients. Sometimes parents are mistakenly feeding toddlers a low-fat diet that is healthy for adults but does not provide enough energy for small children.

Why does diet matter?

A balanced diet provides energy and keeps all the chemical processes in our body working well. Carbohydrates and fats are our main source of energy, but we also need fats for many of the chemical processes in cells. Proteins are used to build muscles and other tissues. Fibre keeps the digestive system working well. Small amounts of vitamins and minerals are really important to keep all the chemical processes working properly. Table 1 shows how much of these food types we need.

You can compare the nutrients in different foods by looking at the '**nutritional information**' labels. Often the label tells you the amount of vitamin or mineral in one serving as a percentage of the **recommended daily amount (RDA)**. If one serving contained 20% of the RDA of vitamin A, you would need to eat five servings to get all the vitamin A you need (if there wasn't any vitamin A in the other food you ate).

Different diets for different people

Our dietary needs change as we get older. Children and adolescents are growing, so they need more protein, to grow new cells, than adults do. Small children are often very active; an average toddler may 'toddle' the equivalent of about 15 km a day. Small children therefore need a higher proportion of high-energy foods, such as fatty foods, than adults do.

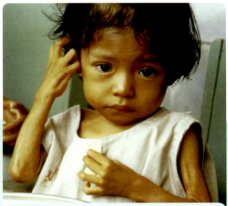

FIGURE 1: Do all malnourished children look like this?

Food type	Proportion of a balanced diet
Carbohydrates	at least 50%
Fats	20–30%
Proteins	25–30%

TABLE 1: Proportion of different food types in a balanced diet.

FIGURE 2: Discuss the dietary needs of the different members of this family.

:: QUESTIONS ::

1 Describe in your own words why a balanced diet is important.

2 Describe why adolescents need to eat more protein than adults.

3 Discuss which would be the better snack for a toddler: some low-fat yoghurt and a small apple, or a piece of cheese and half a banana? Give your reasons.

...dietary recall   ...diet diary   ...electrolytes   ...glycogen

Athletes' needs

FIGURE 3: What do you think these rowers might have eaten just before competing?

Sports nutritionists have to design diets that meet the needs of athletes in different sports, and at different times during training and competing. While athletes are in training, to build extra muscle they are often advised to eat extra protein to provide the 'building blocks' for new cells. The correct training programme ensures that extra muscle is built in the right places.

Just before competing, athletes eat large quantities of foods rich in carbohydrates, such as pasta, rice or bread. These build up stores of **glycogen** in the muscles, which are broken down later to release energy. During hard physical exercise, athletes can be using energy at the equivalent of about 3–4 g of carbohydrates each minute.

During training and competition, athletes also lose water in the form of sweat. Sweat also contains a range of essential minerals, called **electrolytes**. **Isotonic sports drinks** are designed to replace these minerals lost in sweat and also to supply energy. They contain water, glucose and electrolytes.

On average 1 litre of sweat contains these minerals:

calcium	0.02 g
chlorine	1.48 g
magnesium	0.05 g
potassium	0.23 g
sodium	1.15 g

EXAM HINTS AND TIPS

Remember: Isotonic sports drinks contain water, glucose and electrolytes.

Monitoring nutrition

An athlete needs to monitor his or her diet in order to check that they are eating the correct combination of nutrients as recommended by their nutritionist. There are two main ways they do this. The first is to remember and record everything they have eaten in the previous 24 hours (**dietary recall**). The second is to keep a **diet diary** in which the contents of each meal or snack are recorded as they are eaten. If you try either method for long, you will find that athletes need a lot of self-discipline to monitor their diet accurately!

QUESTIONS

4   Describe in your own words why athletes are advised to eat extra protein.

5   Discuss what is meant by 'using energy at the equivalent of 3–4 g of carbohydrates each minute'.

6   Discuss the disadvantages of the methods used to record diet. Can you think of a better method?

EXAM HINTS AND TIPS

Remember: Carbohydrates build up stores of glycogen in the muscles to provide energy.

Diet and injury

FIGURE 4: Can diet prevent or help this?

Tiredness is one of the main causes of injury in top-level athletes. These athletes are usually advised to eat a diet consisting of at least 65% carbohydrates to supply the energy they need, and only 10–15% fat. Fatty foods supply a lot of energy, but they are hard for the body to break down, so they only supply energy slowly. This is appropriate for a low-level sustained effort such as walking, but not for athletes.

When recovering from injury, athletes need a diet relatively low in protein and high in carbohydrates, because only relatively small amounts of protein are needed to repair an injury, and digesting the excess protein uses up energy that is needed to build the protein into new cells.

QUESTIONS

7   Find out more about how athletes use diet to help prevent, and recover from, injury.

Energy for activity

You will find out:
- The basic energy requirements for an active lifestyle
- What athletes eat to provide the energy they need

Antarctic adventure

In November 1992, Sir Ranulph Fiennes and Dr Michael Stroud began a 3-month, unsupported, 2700 km trek across the Antarctic to the South Pole. They underestimated the amount of food they would need to supply the **energy** for all the strenuous physical activity they would be doing, and nearly died. Sir Ranulph lost one-third of his body weight as his body broke down muscle tissue to supply the energy he needed.

FIGURE 1: It is so cold here that ice isn't slippery. The average temperature is about –50° C.

An active lifestyle

You have already learned how the energy you need each day depends on your weight. You can calculate this **basic energy requirement** using the formula:

basic energy requirement per day (in kcal) = weight (in kg) × 24 × 1.3

This formula tells you how much energy you need for an **inactive** lifestyle. But the energy you need each day also depends on how **active** you are; if you are more active, you will need more energy. If you are moderately active, you should calculate your energy requirement using the formula:

energy requirement per day (in kcal) = weight (in kg) × 24 × 1.5

And if you are very active you have to use the formula:

energy requirement per day (in kcal) = weight (in kg) × 24 × 1.75

So if you weigh 60 kg and lead a moderately active lifestyle you will need 2160 kcal each day, as:

energy requirement = 60 × 24 × 1.5 = 2160 kcal

Different sports

Playing some sports makes you tired sooner than others, because different types of sports need different amounts of energy. Figure 3 shows the approximate energy needed each hour to play different sports. So a 40-minute squash session would use about 530 kcal (40 minutes is two-thirds of an hour). Athletes may need up to 7000 kcal per day while they are training or competing.

FIGURE 2: How active is your lifestyle? What sport have you done in the last week?

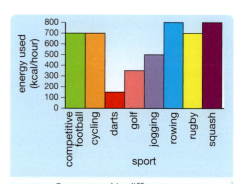

FIGURE 3: Energy used in different sports.

QUESTIONS

1. Which **two** sports from the bar chart in figure 3 use most energy?
2. How much energy would you use for a half-hour jog?
3. Write down the formula to find the energy requirement each day for a very active person.
4. Calculate the energy needed each day by a very active man with a weight of 80 kg.

...active   ...basic energy requirement   ...carbohydrates

Food and energy

Table 1 shows the amount of energy provided by 1 g of different types of food.

Although gram for gram, **fat** provides most energy, it is not a good energy source for athletes because fat takes much longer to digest than **carbohydrates**, so the energy is released much more slowly. Serious athletes aim to get about 60–70% of their daily energy intake from carbohydrates. This usually means eating at least 500 g of carbohydrates a day. Table 2 shows the amount of carbohydrates in different foods.

Food type	Amount of energy provided by 1g
carbohydrate	4 kcal
protein	4 kcal
fat	9 kcal

TABLE 1: Amount of energy provided by different food types.

Food	carbohydrate (g)
medium banana	20
1 pint milk	30
thick slice of bread	30
large tin baked beans	45
large jacket potato	45
large portion of pasta	90

TABLE 2: The amount of carbohydrates in different foods.

Eating for sport

First of all, to provide energy, your body uses the **glucose** in your blood. This is sufficient for 'sprint' activities, such as a 100 m sprint. When this runs out, in 'endurance' activities such as marathon running, your body gets energy from the **glycogen** stored in your muscles and from any stores of fat. Many sports, especially team sports, are a mixture of 'sprint' and 'endurance' activities.

Your body can only store the equivalent of about 300–600 g of carbohydrates as glycogen in muscles, and when you run out of glycogen you very quickly run out of energy. So it is very important for athletes to keep their stores of glycogen 'topped up' during training and competition by eating carbohydrates regularly.

Sports nutritionists recommend that athletes maximise their glycogen stores by eating a meal or snack containing about 75 kcal of carbohydrates three to four hours before exercise. They should also eat plenty of carbohydrates in the four hours following exercise, as this replaces the energy used, aids recovery and 'refuels' the body for the next exercise session.

FIGURE 4: Is rugby a 'sprint' activity or an 'endurance' activity?

Respiratory exchange ratio

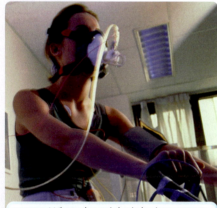

FIGURE 5: What else might it be important to monitor for an athlete?

To assist with training and dietary regimes, an athlete may need to know whether a certain type of exercise is using fat or carbohydrate as its main energy source. Because the chemical reactions involved in breaking down fat and carbohydrate are different, they use different amounts of oxygen and produce different amounts of waste carbon dioxide. Therefore it is possible to tell which reactions are taking place by measuring the oxygen and carbon dioxide levels in the air breathed in and out and calculating the ratio of carbon dioxide produced to oxygen used. A ratio of 0.7 means fat is the energy source, a ratio of 1.0 means carbohydrates are the energy source and between 0.7 and 1.0 means a mixture of fat and carbohydrate is being used.

QUESTIONS

5 Explain why fat is a poor energy source for athletes.

6 List **five** different sports and state whether they are 'sprint' or 'endurance' activities, or both.

7 Explain why athletes eat carbohydrates during training and competition.

8 Suggest a suitable meal or snack for an athlete 3 to 4 hours before exercise.

QUESTIONS

9 An athlete has a ratio of carbon dioxide produced to oxygen used of 0.75. Discuss what this tells you about their exercise and any implications for training and nutrition.

...energy ...fat ...glucose ...glycogen ...inactive

Warm when wet

INVESTIGATION

One material that has made a significant difference to certain types of water sport is neoprene. This is the material that wetsuits are made from, and its purpose is to keep the wearer warm even though both the person and the material are soaking wet.

Tara's group is organising an investigation into neoprene. She writes:

"The way that neoprene insulates someone is to hold the water against the person's skin, but not let the water flow or circulate in any way. This means that as thermal energy from the person's body heats the water up, the warm water is held in place and keeps the body warm. This is why wetsuits have to be tight-fitting – a loose one would allow the warm water to flow away.
The aim of this investigation is to see if the thickness of the neoprene makes any difference to its ability to act as an insulator.

In sports like windsurfing and surfing, you are bound to get very wet. You have to keep warm though, otherwise you wouldn't be able to control your muscle movements in the way that you have to in these sports. People taking part in these sports spend hours being wet and therefore potentially cold and uncomfortable. A good wetsuit, however, will change a miserable experience into a pleasant one and allow the person to focus on and enjoy their sport."

2A.1 Tara has described a vocational application of this investigation and has clearly shown how it relates to her chosen area of sport. To develop the work further, she could incorporate more research into her explanation of why the design of wetsuits is important.

Here is Tara's plan:

The way we are going to do this experiment is to make neoprene of different thicknesses into cup shapes, each one just the right size to snugly fit around a 250 ml beaker. Neoprene is manufactured in thicknesses from 1 mm to 6 mm, going up in 1 mm steps, so we can make six beaker shapes.

The beaker will have warm water put in it. The beaker and water represent the body. There will be a thermometer in the water to enable us to read and record the temperature.

We will put the neoprene sleeves of different thicknesses around the beakers of warm water and stand them in a deep tray of cold water. We will monitor the temperatures to see in which beaker the water cools down quickest. These will represent wetsuited bodies in the sea.

2B.1 Tara has produced a plan which is thought through carefully and could be used by some one else with a little extra guidance. A labelled diagram might help, for example.

Warm when wet

STUDENT'S COMMENTARY

Before doing the experiment, Tara had to complete a risk assessment form given to her by the teacher.

Risk Assessment Form

DESCRIBE THE INVESTIGATION

This investigation involves using glass beakers with water in them and with neoprene around them. We are going to be measuring the temperature of the water in the beaker.

WHAT ARE THE HAZARDS?

There are two hazards in this experiment. The first is that we are going to be using glass beakers and glass thermometers, and the second is that we are going to be using quite a lot of water. It won't be hot but it might get spilt.

WHAT ARE THE RISKS?

The risk from the glass is that if something gets dropped it might break and then someone might get cut with the broken glass. The risk from the water is that if it gets spilt it can make the floor slippery, and that is dangerous if someone were to fall, especially if they were carrying something.

HOW CAN THE RISK BE CONTROLLED?

We will have to be very careful with the glass objects and not drop them or leave them lying around. Thermometers will not be left on a bench top where they might roll off and drop. Any spillages of water will be cleared up straight away and we will have a wet floor warning sign.

WHAT IS THE REMAINING RISK?

If we are careful and sensible with our equipment, then we will most probably be safe.

2B.2 The risk assessment gave some guidance to Tara but she managed to complete it accurately and in detail. She could have achieved a better mark by producing it entirely by herself.

Results

Time (min)	Temperature of water in beaker in 1 mm wet neoprene (°C)	Temperature of water in beaker in 2 mm wet neoprene (°C)	Temperature of water in beaker in 3 mm wet neoprene (°C)	Temperature of water in beaker in 4 mm wet neoprene (°C)	Temperature of water in beaker in 5 mm wet neoprene (°C)	Temperature of water in beaker in 6 mm wet neoprene (°C)
0	40	40	40	40	40	40
1	38	39	40	39	40	40
2	36	38	39	38	39	39
3	33	37	37	37	38	39
4	31	35	36	36	37	38
5	29	33	34	35	36	37
6	28	31	33	34	35	36
7	27	29	31	32	34	35
8	25	28	30	31	33	34
9	24	27	29	30	32	33
10	23	26	28	29	31	32

3C.1 Tara showed that she could select suitable equipment, set it up appropriately and extract a good set of results that showed a clear pattern. The results were appropriately displayed, but she could have further improved her mark by considering the role of repeated readings.

What the results show

The experiment did show the results we expected – that the thicker the neoprene, the more effectively it insulates the container. The temperature drops more slowly if the neoprene is thicker and there is a clear relationship between the thickness of the neoprene and the final temperature.

2D.1 The results were processed effectively to show a pattern and support a conclusion. Tara could develop the conclusion further by going into more detail, such as whether beyond a certain thickness, neoprene might still insulate better if the thickness continues to increase.

Using the results

This was a good experiment and quite clearly showed that neoprene is more effective when it's thicker. The results would prove to a sports scientist that thicker neoprene is a better insulator. They might know this already, but it would help to prove it to customers. Winter weight wetsuits are thicker for this reason. In the winter, the sea is colder and so you lose body heat quicker. However, the sleeves of wetsuits are not usually quite as thick. This is because you lose less heat through your arms than through your body. Also, the thicker the neoprene, the harder it is to move your arms, so it is better to have it not quite as thick.

2E.1 Tara has evaluated the experimental procedures. She could explain in more detail how the data could be made more reliable.

Up and up

You will find out:

● About different sports materials

● What properties make these materials the best for these uses

Better materials mean better performances

Pole vaulters used to use bamboo poles that were flexible but strong, and also light. But then they started using aluminium. Aluminium is a low-density metal, so the poles could still be strong and quite light. Later a new kind of **composite** material became available, which was strong and light but also very flexible. It changed the vaulters' technique and allowed records to be broken.

The right properties

A vaulting pole needs to be light to make it easy to run with. So the material it is made of must have low **density**. It must also have **strength**, so that it doesn't snap when it bends.

The top athletes have poles made just for them, matched to their weight. A heavier person needs a stiffer pole or it will bend too much. A lighter person needs a more flexible pole.

Density, strength and **flexibility** are all properties of materials.

Bamboo is a natural material that athletes used a hundred years ago, but it wasn't always reliable. Aluminium is a metal, and for many years it was the best material for making poles. It has plenty of strength but its flexibility and density are not perfect.

Poles are now made of a composite material that takes advantage of the properties of different materials combined together. **Polymer** material provides flexibility and low density. Polymers are substances like nylon and polypropylene. Carbon fibres embedded in the polymer add strength.

FIGURE 1: New materials mean new records.

WANT TO KNOW MORE?

Find out more about Olympic records at
http://www.olympic.org/uk/utilities/reports/level2_uk.asp?HEAD2=10&HEAD1=5

QUESTIONS

1 Why must a pole be light?

2 What property of a material allows the pole to be light?

3 Steel is strong. Why don't athletes use steel poles?

4 What is the advantage of using a composite material?

...composite ...compressive strength ...density ...flexibility

Storing energy

Pole vaulters use the energy of the run-up to bend the pole. The bent pole acts as an energy store. It gives the energy back to the athlete to lift them over the high bar. Good jumping is all about good technique in bending the pole, and then getting the energy back from it to go skywards in the most efficient way.

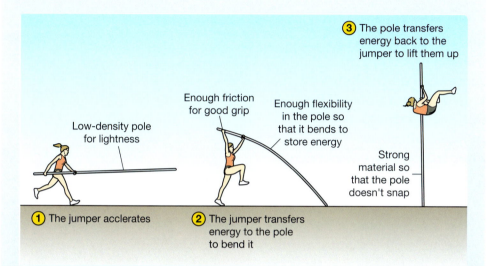

③ The pole transfers energy back to the jumper to lift them up

Enough friction for good grip

Enough flexibility in the pole so that it bends to store energy

Low-density pole for lightness

Strong material so that the pole doesn't snap

① The jumper acclerates

② The jumper transfers energy to the pole to bend it

FIGURE 2: The athlete stores energy in the motion of her own body, and then transfers the energy to the pole. The bent pole acts as a new energy store. It transfers energy back to the athlete to lift them up.

The record of records

Sports scientists help athletes to improve by developing equipment that is made of the right materials with the right properties. Table 1 shows what has happened to men's Olympic records in pole vaulting since the very first modern games in 1896. The record has gone up and up.

Year	1896	1900	1908	1912	1920	1928	1932	1936	1952
Height (m)	3.30	3.30	3.71	3.95	4.09	4.20	4.31	4.32	4.55
Year	1956	1960	1964	1968	1972	1980	1988	1996	2004
Height (m)	4.56	4.70	5.10	5.40	5.50	5.78	5.90	5.92	5.95

TABLE 1: Olympic records for pole vaulting, 1896 to 2004

Scratches can hurt

Vaulting poles *can* snap, even though they are built to bend. The problem is worse if there are scratches on the surface. The scratches provide starting points for fractures.

All of this shows that 'strength' is a hard **property** to define and measure. A material can have **tensile strength**, which is a measure of how easily it breaks when stretched. It also has **compressive strength**, which tells us how much a material can be squashed. Glass, for example, has high compressive strength, but much lower tensile strength. And the tensile strength is not fixed, but depends on the existence of scratches, which provide starting points for fractures to run through the material. The presence of carbon fibres in a composite material greatly increases tensile strength, but that doesn't mean that vaulting poles can't snap when mistreated.

...polymer   ...property   ...strength   ...tensile strength

Tennis technology

You will find out:

- About some natural and synthetic materials and their different properties
- About the importance of friction and equipment design

Racquets for everybody

If you are a leading tennis player then there is plenty of choice of racquets to suit your playing style. And if you are an ordinary player then you, too, probably need all the help you can get from the equipment. One type of racquet has a large head, to make it easier to hit the ball. Such racquets would have been impossible not that many years ago. The development of new, low-**density** but strong materials has made the difference.

Racquets

Thirty years ago, tennis racquets were made of wood. It's a **natural** composite material, made of fibres embedded in a solid. Strings could be natural too, made of animal gut, or they could be **synthetic**. A synthetic material is made by human technologies.

When steel racquets came along, they proved to be winners in the hands of a top player who could handle the extra weight. For ordinary players, though, they were too heavy. The weight problem was solved by racquets made with graphite and foam – a synthetic **composite** material. These made it possible to have racquets with 'ultra big heads'. They made it easier for ordinary players to hit the ball.

In general, materials for making tennis racquets should have these properties:

- Low density, so that racquets are not too heavy.
- High **tensile strength**, so that structure can be slender without breaking.
- **Flexible**, but not too flexible, so that the strings can be at the right tightness and the ball has the right amount of bounce.

FIGURE 1: Whether you're the world's best player or not, there is a tennis racquet that has the right technology to match how you play.

Shoes

Tennis shoes must grip the ground firmly, so soles with good treads are needed to provide the right amount of friction. Friction makes it harder for one surface to slide across another. Smooth soles would be a disaster on court.

A player must also accelerate and decelerate, jump and land. The soles of shoes have to absorb the 'shock' of all that landing on the ground, especially on hard-court surfaces. A player's legs will feel the strain without shoes that help to absorb the shock. So shoe design is 'hi-tech', just as for racquets.

QUESTIONS

1 What kind of material is best for making large but lightweight rackets?
2 Friction is important for shoes. Where on a tennis racket is it important to have friction to prevent sliding?

EXAM HINTS AND TIPS

Remember: A material that has been created by human technologies out of natural raw materials is a 'synthetic' material.

...composite ...density ...flexible

Elements and alloys

Titanium and aluminium are elements. Iron is another element - it's a substance that you can't split into simpler substances. However, steel is an alloy. It is made up of elements (including iron) mixed together, so it is not an element itself. It's not a single 'pure' substance.

Titanium

Titanium is a strong metal that is much less dense than steel. The densities of titanium, steel and aluminium are:

titanium	4500 kg/m^3
steel	7800 kg/m^3
aluminium	2700 kg/m^3

Titanium can also be mixed with other metals, and non-metals too, to make alloys. Titanium alloys are very useful for making structures, including tennis racquets, that combine lightness with strength.

Properties of metals

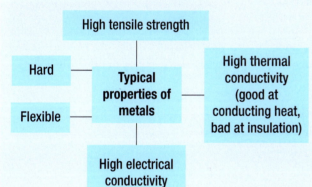

FIGURE 2: Titanium or titanium alloy tennis racquet.

WANT TO KNOW MORE?

Find out more about tennis technology at:
http://news.bbc.co.uk/sportacademy/hi/sa/tennis/features/newsid_3003000/3003188.stm

Kevlar®

Kevlar® is used to make bullet-proof vests, and for making some tennis racquets. It's a polymer that is spun in pretty much the same way as a spider spins its web or a silkworm makes silk. The fibres are made of long molecular chains, with a name to match: polyparaphenylene terephthalamide. The extreme strength of the material, and its resistance to heat, comes from the links between the chains.

FIGURE 3: Bullet-proof vest.

QUESTIONS

3 Aluminium is less dense than either steel or titanium. Suggest why it is not used on its own for making tennis racquet frames.

4 Picture two tennis racquets of the same size and shape, one made from steel and the other from titanium.
 a Which one is heavier?
 b Is the heavier one more or less than twice as heavy?

5 Explain why using a less dense material allows bigger racquets to be used.

6 The density data can be shown on a pie chart or a bar chart – which is best? Sketch your preferred representation, showing the data.

QUESTIONS

7 Find out about other polymers with links between the chain molecules. How do the links influence the material's properties?

...natural ...synthetic ...tensile strength

A matter of survival

You will find out:

- Why polymers are good materials for light and comfortable sports clothing, and how they compare with natural fibres
- That thermal insulation is an important requirement in extreme conditions

Not for wimps

Mountain marathons are not for wimps. Runners have to carry everything they need for two days in the mountains. They need food, good clothing, and they even have to carry their own shelter, bedding and cooking equipment. In the high and exposed hills, the weather can throw anything at them – rain, hail, sleet or snow. Good preparation makes the difference between winning and losing. It's also a matter of survival.

Running in the mountains

A human body must stay at the same temperature. Under normal conditions it is pretty good at doing that for itself. It sweats to cool down, it shivers and it burns food to keep warm. But in high mountain extremes it needs all the help it can get.

For a start it must have fuel, or food, so mountain marathon runners have to make sure they carry enough food. High-energy foods like pasta, rice and cake are all good. The body will burn them all.

For running in the mountains, clothing needs to be light, insulating and weatherproof. It must allow the body to sweat when it is working hard going uphill. So runners use a polymer layer next to the skin which is a good thermal insulator. It helps to slow down energy loss and so it keeps the runner warm, but fine droplets of sweat can get through it, so that the wind quickly carries moisture away and the dampness doesn't build up. A sweaty cotton T-shirt is a big problem when the body eases up. It can quickly make the runner get cold – very cold.

Spandex is a good example of a hi-tech material that is useful for runners. It is very stretchy, flexible, and light. It is also quite good at thermal insulation. One brand name for spandex is Lycra®.

FIGURE 1: Mountain marathon competitors.

Watch Out Thermal insulators don't do anything to make you get warmer. They don't supply extra energy to your body. They just make it harder for energy to escape.

EXAM HINTS AND TIPS

Remember: Thermal means to do with temperature and heating. So thermal conductivity of a material is how good it is at conducting heat.

QUESTIONS

1. Why do mountain marathon runners need to make sure that they eat a lot?
2. Why is thermal insulation so important?
3. Why can sweating be dangerous?

...density   ...energy   ...flexibility   ...fuel   ...insulation

Layering

Mountain marathon runners and people working in extreme conditions, such as in the Antarctic, need to take a careful approach to clothing. They need to build up three layers, each with its own job to do.

Fabric made from polypropylene is a good material for the bottom layer of clothing, or the base layer. It stretches, it has low density and its flexibility makes it comfortable. It is also a good thermal insulator. Very importantly, its fibres help to carry moisture away from the skin so that dampness is less likely to build up.

A fleece layer goes on top of the base layer, for good insulation. Its polyester fabric and the fluffy structure that traps air make it light as well as insulating. And because it's light and flexible, and usually has a full-length zip, it is easy to take on and off so that the runner can control their heat loss.

The outer layer has to be waterproof and windproof. A body soaked in rain or melted snow cools down quickly and dangerously.

FIGURE 2: What three layers do people in extreme cold need?.

Heroic failure

Captain Robert Scott led an expedition to the South Pole in 1911–12. Wearing clothes made of wool and cotton, they reached their destination, the end of the world. But struggling to pull their sledges home, even in temperatures of –50° C, they sweated. Inevitably in such Antarctic conditions, the sweat froze. When they got into their fur sleeping bags at night, the ice melted, drenching everything. The next morning they had only their wet clothes to put back on again, to face another round of freezing. They all suffered the pain of frostbite, which can cause loss of fingers and toes. Bravely, they tried to get back to the ocean. But none of them made it.

FIGURE 3: Captain Robert Scott and his team.

QUESTIONS

4   Draw a sketch to show how the three layers of clothing work together to protect the wearer from rapid energy loss.

5   Use scientific language to explain why wet clothing is dangerous in extreme conditions.

QUESTIONS

6   Human body temperature is approximately 37° C. Explain why the difference between body temperature and the temperature of the surroundings is critically important.

...polymer   ...polypropylene   ...temperature   ...thermal insulator

The right stuff

You will find out:
- About how material properties are matched to their uses in a motor sport
- About ceramic materials and their properties

Courage plus technology

There is no doubting the courage of a motorbike racer. You have to be made of the right stuff to go out there and compete at speed. You also need the right back-up from the team who support you on race days. Back-up also comes from all the people who have developed the technologies. That includes all the hi-tech materials that your bike is made from, and all the hi-tech materials that you are wearing. Motorbike racers need the right stuff.

FIGURE 1: Both this biker's bike and his helmet are 'hi-tech' in many ways.

Speed, safety and comfort

Obviously speed counts in races, but so do safety and comfort. The biker's clothing, the helmet and the bike itself are all 'hi-tech'. That means the materials they are made from are complicated, and specially made for such uses.

The clothing is made from special **polymers**. The inner layers provide good **insulation** and carry moisture away from the skin, so that the biker doesn't become wet with sweat. Most of the outer surface is smooth for low **friction** and **streamlining**. Air can flow smoothly across it and, if the rider makes contact with the ground, the material doesn't scratch and catch easily.

The helmet has a **composite** structure. It's made of different materials combined together, to get the benefits of their combined properties. It has carbon fibres and very tough Kevlar® embedded in solid resin. The resin has **low density** and just the right amount of flexibility, while the carbon fibres and Kevlar® provide strength.

In the bike itself, thermal insulation is a big issue. The exhaust system is right under the driver's seat, and that could cause some serious overheating problems! The exhaust itself has an outer surface with a large **surface area**, so that energy can transfer quickly to the air. A layer of modern **ceramic** material protects the rider. These materials can have a low density, so they don't add too much to the mass of the bike. The biggest advantage of ceramic materials is their low **thermal conduction** and their high **temperature resistance**.

QUESTIONS

1 Make a simple sketch of a biker and bike. Add labels to your sketch to show: a composite material; a low-density material; a good thermal insulator (to reduce rate of energy transfer); a large surface area (to increase rate of energy transfer); a ceramic material; a material with fibres embedded in resin.
   Hint: You can mention the same material more than once.

...ceramic   ...composite   ...friction   ...insulation   ...low density   ...matrix   ...polymers

Composite sense

What natural material would be good for making bikers' helmets? Wood? Strong but not strong enough, splintering dangerously in an accident. Lead? Not bad at absorbing impact if it's thick enough, but much too dense. So what about manufactured steel? Too stiff to absorb much energy in a crash, and still too dense. Synthetic composites provide the answer.

A composite material normally has a solid **matrix**, such as resin (a polymer material that acts like hardened glue). Embedded in the matrix are other materials, '**reinforcing**' materials, which add strength. Fibreglass is a composite material, with fibres of glass adding surprising strength to the resin matrix. Wood is a natural composite, with fibres of cellulose stuck tight together in a matrix of a substance called lignin.

Even concrete is a composite, with a matrix of set cement holding small stones or gravel together. The material is much, much stronger than the cement would be on its own.

WANT TO KNOW MORE?

Find out more about composite materials at
http://www.science.org.au/nova/059/059key.htm

FIGURE 2: What material?

EXAM HINTS AND TIPS

Remember: Thermal conduction is the opposite of thermal insulation. A good conductor is a bad insulator.

Advanced synthetic composites

In advanced synthetic composites, the matrix is usually a polymer. However, carbon, ceramics and even metals can be used for the matrix. Ceramics, for example, are useful for applications in which very high heat resistance is important, as in an engine. Fibres of glass are the most common reinforcement in composite materials, but carbon fibres are also used. They are more expensive but they make stronger composite materials, so they are good for uses such as tennis racquets and golf clubs.

QUESTIONS

2 Reinforced concrete is even stronger than regular concrete. Use the Internet to find out why.

3 Find **three** different uses for fibreglass and explain why its properties make it suitable for each use.

4 Draw up a table with rows for polymer, ceramic and metal. Make columns for strength, flexibility, thermal conductivity and density. Use the table to create a summary of the properties of the three types of material.

QUESTIONS

5 Find out about a use of a ceramic as a matrix in a composite material **or** about the use of composites in aircraft construction.

...reinforcing   ...streamlining   ...surface area   ...temperature resistance   ...thermal conduction

Breathable cloth?

INVESTIGATION

This investigation is about testing a manufacturer's claims for a type of material. Scientists are sometimes involved with work of this kind, in which a material is to be tested in terms of suitability for a particular application. In this case, the material is Gore-Tex, which is used to make waterproof clothing for sporting activities such as climbing and hiking.

Phil carried out an investigation with his team to test claims that vapour could escape, but that water can't pass through the material. He wrote:

"Gore-Tex has a particularly property in that it will let water vapour out but won't let water in. It does this by having a mesh with a particular size of hole. Water droplets are much bigger than the holes, but the molecules of water in water vapour are much smaller. This means that water vapour produced by the body from physical activity can escape but rain can't enter.

We tested Gore-Tex to see whether water vapour could pass through it but not water, even with some force. We designed two tests, one to test whether water vapour passed through and the second to test whether water did. The reason so many people use Gore-Tex is because they want to do something like fell walking, where you get hot and sweaty by working hard. They want the moisture to escape, but if it's raining they don't want to get wet. This is important for a sports scientist, because such materials could give you an advantage in competitions or just make things better for you in your sport."

3A.1 Phil has carried out some research into how Gore-Tex works, so he has been able to include some scientific ideas about the mesh and the comparative size of molecules. He has also explained how the application of this will be useful to people involved in selecting equipment for planning activities. He could further develop his work by including diagrams to explain his ideas about how the material works.

Here is Phil's plan for the water test:

Waterproof clothing should be waterproof even when the rain is severe, so we wanted to find a way of testing this. What we did was to design an experiment that would simulate a downpour.

We fitted material covers (three Gore-Tex and three polythene) to six 250 ml beakers as in the water vapour test. The beakers were stood in a shower cubicle and the shower turned on hard and cold and left for half an hour. At the end of that time, the shower was turned off and the beakers examined to see if any water had penetrated through to them.

Here is Phil's plan for vapour test:

The way we did this was to use a piece of Gore-Tex to seal a beaker with water inside it. The water was kept at body temperature so that it simulated the way in which moisture on the surface of the body evaporates. The water was maintained at 38°C by using a water bath. We weighed the beaker, water, Gore-Tex and elastic band before and afterwards. This told us what the weight loss was, but we had to be careful to dry the outside of the beaker carefully, because it had been standing in water and this could have altered the weight.

First we set up a water bath at 38°C. We got nine 250 ml beakers and put 200 ml of water in each. Then we put a piece of Gore-Tex material over the top of three of the beakers and a piece of polythene over another three, and secured them with tight elastic bands. We weighed the beakers and then put them in the water bath, taking care not to let the coverings come in contact with the water in the water bath. We left the apparatus and every hour removed the beakers, weighed them and returned them.

3B.1 Phil has clearly set out a logical plan which could be easily and effectively carried out by someone else. The steps are clear and appropriate to the experiment; they could have been further enhanced by a labelled diagram.

Breathable cloth?

STUDENT'S COMMENTARY

Before we carried out the experiment, we summarised what we saw as possible hazards and explained how we would avoid them. This was checked by our teacher before we started work.

Risk Assessment Form

DESCRIPTION OF MY INVESTIGATION
We are going to do two experiments as part of our investigation. The first of these will be done by putting some beakers in a shower. The beakers will have lids, some polythene and some Gore-Tex. The purpose is to see if the lids will let water through. The second experiment also involves using beakers, but this time we are going to stand them in a water bath.

WHAT ARE THE HAZARDS?
The thing that could be dangerous about the first experiment is that we will have water showering down on glass, which will make it slippery. The water could also make the floor slippery if it is split onto it. There is a hazard in the second experiment because the beakers will be wet when they come out, and this will make them slippery.

WHAT ARE THE RISKS?
The risk in the first experiment is that if a beaker were to get slippery, we could drop it and it could break and, especially in a shower where people will be standing with bare feet, this could lead to people cutting themselves. If water spilt onto the floor, it could make it slippery and people could fall over and hurt themselves. The risk in the second experiment is that, when the beakers become slippery, someone could drop them and they could break.

HOW CAN THE RISK BE CONTROLLED?
We will reduce the risk for the first experiment by standing the beakers in a tray with a perforated base, so that the water can run through. This means that we will put the tray of beakers in the shower and lift it out instead of handling the beakers. This will make the experiment safer and make breakage much less likely. We will clear up any spilt water straight away. What we will do to make the second experiment safer is to lift the beakers out at the end of the time in the water bath and dry and weigh them on the same bench, so that we don't have to carry them across the room.

WHAT IS THE REMAINING RISK?
If we use these precautions then both experiments can be made safe.

3B.2 Phil carried out an assessment of the risks from this experiment and identified what control measures had to be put in place. The teacher approved this; he could have included these details in the plan for the benefit of other students.

What we found out
The vapour test

This table showed that:

Hours	Average mass of beakers with Gore-Tex lid (g)	Average mass of beakers with polythene lid (g)	Average mass of beakers with no lid (g)
0	438	429	414
1	437	429	412
2	436	429	409
3	434	429	407
4	433	429	405
5	431	429	402
6	430	429	400

- In beakers with a Gore-Tex lid the mass dropped gradually as water evaporated and escaped through the Gore-Tex.
- In beakers with a polythene lid the mass remained unchanged. Even though some of the water had evaporated, it had been unable to escape through the non-permeable polythene and had condensed there.
- In beakers with no lid the mass had dropped gradually as the water had evaporated and escaped.

The greater loss of mass from beakers with no lid was due to the fact that the vapours could circulate more easily there than in beakers with Gore-Tex where there was a lid.

The water test

After 30 minutes of continuous showering, none of the beakers had allowed any water to permeate at all; the Gore-Tex as well as the polythene was effectively waterproof.

The overall conclusion we came to was that Gore-Tex will allow vapours to escape but will stop water from passing through. It will therefore very successfully function as a material for garments in sports such as hiking, in which moisture from the body needs to be dissipated and yet protection from rain needs to be assured.

3C.1 Phil has selected and used equipment appropriate to the investigation and capable of producing useful results. The results have been processed in a way that is appropriate and which show the underlying pattern. Both of the experiments involved averaging a number of results and the overall trend does not indicate the need to gather more data.

3D.1 Phil has used the results to produce conclusions that are well-formed and related to the investigation. He could have related it more closely to the ideas about the structure of the material.

Evaluation

I think we were successful in both of our experiments in modelling the conditions in which Gore-Tex is supposed to function. The vapour test showed that vapour produced at body temperature can pass through the material relatively easily. The water test put the material into the kind of situation a waterproof material would have to cope with, but we could have extended it in length as someone wearing this kind of clothing might have been in the rain for hours, not just 30 minutes.

The investigation we did was very much what a sports scientist might do to test the suitability of material for a particular application."

2E.1 Phil has evaluated the procedure they used and suggested an improvement. He could go into this and the use of these findings in more detail.

Fitness, sports clothing and energy requirements

Mike and Suhail had to run to the bus stop in the morning to catch the bus to school. On the bus they argued about who was fit and who was out of shape. Mike reckoned that if Will was more exhausted after they had run the same distance, he was less fit. Will thought that Mike's inability to keep up showed that he was less fit. Mike said he was fit but just couldn't be bothered to run for the bus.

How could you design an investigation that involved people doing the same amount of exercise and then measuring their recovery rate? What kind of activity could you use? What does 'recovery rate' mean and how can it be measured? Would this be a way of deciding which of the boys was the fittest?

Jemima and Debbie have decided to investigate the effect of friction burns on different types of sportswear materials. They know that sportswear has to be lightweight if worn indoors to avoid people overheating. They wanted to see whether all kinds of fabric were equally prone to damage or whether some were worse than others.

The teacher suggested that they should design a piece of equipment to test fabrics by friction. Something would have to rub against the material and do so in a way that was repeatable, so that all the fabrics were tested in the same way. What do you think they might set up that could 'friction test' fabrics in a fair way? How could this equipment then be used to decide which fabric was better at resisting that kind of damage?

Pete, Sean and Hiten are planning to hike across Dartmoor in the autumn. They will be carrying their camping gear and food with them. They are planning walking around 15 km each day and will be out for four days. The weather is likely to be fairly cold, windy and possibly wet, but if it looks severe they will come off the moor.

Estimate their energy requirements and suggest what their diet might include, remembering that they have no cold storage and any cooking will have to be done using a portable camping stove.

Sarah plays tennis a lot and sees that in her local sportswear shop they have a new range of socks that claim to be absorbent. She knows that when playing tennis hard her feet can get sweaty, so she thinks this is a good idea but decides to test it out. However, it occurs to her that a manufacturer might make socks more absorbent by making them thicker. If they're too thick she won't be able to get her shoes on. How could she test different types of socks to see which are the most absorbent, while avoiding ones that are too bulky?

Rachel is planning to run a marathon. It will be her first attempt at a run of such a distance and she has a carefully planned training schedule over the next three months. She wants to keep a record of measurements that will show the changes taking place in her body during the training. Propose a set of variables that she could measure, explain how the measurements could be made and predict what they will show over the period of preparation.

What should I include?

To complete your investigation you need to:

- explain how your investigation can help to run an effective test

- produce a plan that is detailed enough for someone else to be able to follow

- carry out a risk assessment

- decide what equipment to use in your investigation

- carry out your plan carefully and collect and record your results

- process your results and explain your conclusions

- evaluate your investigation, explaining its strengths and weaknesses

- explain how your findings can be used as part of the sports and fitness industry.

Unit summary

Concept map

Your triceps and biceps are examples of antagonistic muscles.

Lungs transfer oxygen from the air you breathe in into the blood, and carbon dioxide from the blood into the air you breathe out.

Insulin makes the liver absorb glucose out of the blood. Glucagon stimulates the liver to release glucose back into the blood.

The diaphragm and the intercostal muscles move air in and out of the lungs.

Exercise and the human body

Anaerobic respiration is the breaking down of glucose molecules without using oxygen.

The heart pumps blood to deliver oxygen, glucose and other nutrients to all parts of the body. Blood also carries waste products, like carbon dioxide, so that the body can get rid of them.

During exercise, the body keeps cool by sweating and also by increasing the diameter of small blood vessels (capillaries) just under the skin.

Aerobic respiration uses glucose and oxygen to supply energy.

Food, together with oxygen, provides energy to the body. Daily energy requirements are different for different people.

Protein in food helps to build muscle.

Sports nutrition

Isotonic sports drinks contain water, glucose and electrolytes.

Complex carbohydrates help the body to build up a good glycogen store in the muscles before exercise.

A material with high thermal conductivity is good at transferring energy through it.

Materials for sport

Composite materials combine the benefits of properties of different materials.

A material with high tensile strength does not break easily when stretched.

Properties of ceramics include high melting point and low thermal conductivity.

Metals have high tensile strength, high thermal conductivity, flexibility and hardness. These are 'properties' of metals.

Density is 'lightness for size'.

The properties of polymers include low density, flexibility and low thermal conductivity.

Unit quiz

1   What part does haemoglobin play in the process of respiration?

2   What part of the body does the term 'cardio' refer to?

3   Name an antagonistic pair of muscles in the human body.

4   Aerobic respiration involves a chemical reaction between two substances. What are they called?

5   Anaerobic respiration involves the break-up of molecules of one substance. What is it called?

6   What is measured in units called kilocalories and kilojoules?

7   What is 'recovery rate'?

8   Water content is one factor that the body works to keep the same. Name **two** more.

9   What do insulin and glucagon do?

10 What does body mass index (BMI) measure?

11 In the human body, what main purposes do **a)** carbohydrates and **b)** proteins have?

12 Which is better for making the shaft of a golf club: wood or steel? Why?

13 What benefits do composite materials provide for making golf club shafts?

14 Why is polypropylene better than cotton for the clothing of a marathon runner?

15 Give an example, from motor racing, of the use of a material **a)** with high thermal conductivity and **b)** with low thermal conductivity.

16 What is density and why is it important in the design of sports materials?

17 Give examples, from any sport, of the use of **a)** high-friction surfaces and **b)** low-friction surfaces.

Citizenship activity

Scientific research has shown that sport is good for health. Active people have fewer health problems, and on average they live for longer. However, people don't do sport just for their health. They do it mainly because it is fun. It can be fun because it involves being with other people, socialising. Or it can be fun because of the satisfaction of competition, the satisfaction of trying (and, occasionally, of doing well or even winning). But a lot of people drop out of sport after they leave school.

QUESTIONS

1   In what ways is sport good for health?

2   Where can you find scientific data that supports the idea that sport is good for health?

3   Suggest why some people give up sport after they leave school.

4   Do you think it matters whether people drop out of sport?

5   Some people discover 'unusual' sports, like archery or climbing, after they leave school. Do you think that schools should allow people to try a wider range of sports? Would that be possible?

Exam practice

 1 Glucose and oxygen are both important during exercise.

  a Where does your body get its oxygen from? [1]
  b How does the oxygen travel around your body? [1]
  c How does your body increase the rate of supply of oxygen to muscles during exercise? Mention two ways. [2]
  d Where does your body get its glucose from? [1]
  e What does your body do to glucose if there is too much in your blood? [1]
  f How does your body make glucose available quickly when you exercise? [1]

 2 Your body's temperature, water content and glucose concentration vary very little.

  a What can your body do if its temperature starts to fall? [2]
  b What can your body do if its temperature starts to become too high? [2]
  c How does your body prevent its water content from rising too high? [2]
  d What can your body do to keep its glucose concentration as high as it should be? [2]
  e What does your body do if your glucose concentration is too high? [1]

 3 These data show levels of healthiness of different resting heart rates for women aged 20 to 29:

Excellent	Good	Fair	Poor
70 or less	71 to 76	77 to 94	95 or more

These data show levels of healthiness of different heart rates 30 seconds after exercise, for the same people:

Excellent	Good	Fair	Poor
86 or less	87 to 92	93 to 109	110 or more

  a Why are the values in the second table higher than the values in the first table? [3]
  b Present the information in the tables in visual form. You could use bar charts or any other format that you think will work. Label your visual presentation so that the information is as clear as possible. [3]

 4 The top pie chart presents information about the ideal balance of three food types in a healthy diet.

A good diet should also contain small amounts of minerals and vitamins, and water is also essential.

The bottom pie chart presents information about different types of substance in the human body.

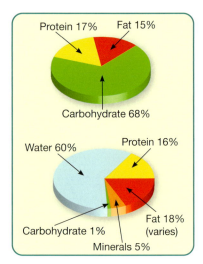

  a Which should you eat more of: fat or protein? [1]
  b Name an important mineral in the human body. Say where it is found. [2]
  c If you keep eating protein, why doesn't the amount of protein in your body keep increasing? [1]
  d Draw a bar chart to compare the percentage of carbohydrate in a balanced diet and the percentage of carbohydrate in a human body. [2]
  e Explain why very little of the body is carbohydrate, but carbohydrate makes up most of the food we eat. [3]

 5 The following lists are of various types of sports equipment and their features.

Sports equipment	Equipment features
Skis	High thermal insulation
Vaulting poles	Good at absorbing shock
Shot (for putting)	Low-friction surfaces
Climbing rope	Flexibility
Wetsuit	High density
Mountain jacket	High tensile strength
Road running shoes	Low density

  a Draw up a table matching the equipment to its features. [7]
  b A putting shot is made from metal. Say whether the material used is:

    i   natural or synthetic [1]
    ii a single material or a composite material [1]

(Total 40 marks)

Worked example

The table gives the tensile strengths and densities of various materials:

Material	Water	Wood (oak)	Nylon	Glass-reinforced polyester	Concrete	Aluminium	Steel
Tensile strength (Pa)	–	21 million	70 million	100 million	Low	250 million	1000 million
Density (kg/m³)	1000	720	1130	1750	2300	2700	7750

a   Name one composite material from the table. [1]

b   Use the data in the table to help you answer the following questions.

   i   Which is the densest material?   [1]
   ii   Which one is the least dense?   [1]
   iii   Suggest why glass-reinforced polyester might be a good material to use for vaulting poles.   [1]

iv   What extra information about the properties of glass-reinforced polyester would you need in order to decide if it is suited to this use?   [1]

v   Use the data to explain whether or not materials with a high tensile strength always have a high density.   [1]

Correct. It is made by combining two or more raw materials.

Incorrect. You have looked up tensile strength and not density.

Correct. It has fairly high tensile strength compared with density. To answer this you have to think about the required properties for a vaulting pole. You have to understand the data.

Good answer.

a   Glass-reinforced polyester

b i   Steel

ii   Concrete

iii   It is quite strong but light.

iv   You would need to know about flexibility.

v   For all of the materials, the higher the tensile strength, the higher the density.

Correct. You read across the density row in the table and find the highest figure.

Wrong. There is no direct relationship between the properties. Look at concrete, for example. It has low tensile strength but quite high density. You have to look at all the data and see if you can spot any relationship. (Graphs are useful for helping you to spot relationships, though there is no *need* to plot a graph here.)

Overall mark awarded: B

How to get an A

You need to know what a composite material is and you need to work out that a vaulting pole needs to be flexible. For the rest of the marks, you should take information carefully from the table. The final part of the question is the real tester – you have to look to see if there is a pattern in the data.

Functions of vitamins and minerals

Vitamin A	healthy eyesight, keeps mucous membranes free from infection
Vitamin B	release of energy from carbohydrate foods, nerve functions
Vitamin D	healthy teeth and bones, absorption of calcium and phosphorus
Vitamin K	aids the clotting of blood
Vitamin C	maintenance of the immune system, absorption of iron, maintenance of skin and linings of the digestive system
Iron	helps the body to manufacture haemoglobin, which is responsible for transporting oxygen around the body
Calcium	for healthy teeth and bones
Phosphorus	aids release of energy from food
Zinc	for enzyme action and wound healing

Energy content of different nutrients

Nutrient	Energy content (kJ/g)
carbohydrate	16
protein	17
fat	38

Basic daily energy requirements (BER)

For every kg of body mass, 1.3 Kcal are required every hour.

If your body mass is 60kg, you will require 78 Kcal every hour, or 1872 Kcal per day.

Body Mass Index

$$BMI = \frac{\text{weight (in kg)}}{\text{height (in m)}^2}$$

If your weight is 55kg and your height is 155cm, your BMI is 22.9.

Types of food additives

Type of additive	What they do
Antioxidants	Make food last longer, increase shelf life.
Flavourings	'Bring out' the flavour of some foods.
Colourings	Make food colourful, either because the food has lost its natural colour during processing or because manufacturers think it will look nice.
Preservatives	Stop food 'going off' and make it last longer.
Sweeteners	Alternative to sugar. They have a lower energy content and are often much sweeter than sugar.
Thickeners	Give 'body' to food.

FORENSIC SCIENCE

Refractive index

$$\text{refractive index} = \frac{\sin I}{\sin R}$$

Blood groups

Blood group	A	B	AB	O
Antigens on red cells	A	B	A and B	None
Antibodies in plasma	anti B	anti A	none	anti A and anti B

Properties on ionic compounds

- They have high melting points
- They have high boiling points
- They tend to be soluble in water

Properties of simple molecules

- They have low melting and boiling points and are often liquids or gases at room temperature
- They are usually insoluble in water, although they may dissolve in other liquids

Precipitates formed with sodium hydroxide

Metal ion	Colour of precipitate
Calcium (Ca^{2+})	White
Copper (Cu^{2+})	Blue
Iron (Fe^{2+})	Grey-green
Iron (Fe^{3+})	Fox-brown

Simple covalent compounds and their formulae

Carbon dioxide	CO_2
Water	H_2O
Ethanol	C_2H_5OH
Glucose	$C_6H_{12}O_6$

Flame test colours

Metal ion	Colour of flame
Sodium ($Na+$)	Yellow-orange
Potassium (K^+)	Lilac
Calcium (Ca^{2+})	Brick-red
Copper (Cu^{2+})	Blue-green

SPORTS SCIENCE

Equation for Aerobic respiration

glucose + oxygen → carbon dioxide + water + energy

$$C_6H_{12}O_6 + 6O_2 \rightarrow 6CO_2 + 6H_2O + 2900 \text{ kJ}$$

Equation for anaerobic respiration

glucose → lactic acid + energy

$$C_6H_{12}O_6 \rightarrow 2C_3H_6O_3 + 120 \text{ kJ}$$

Glossary

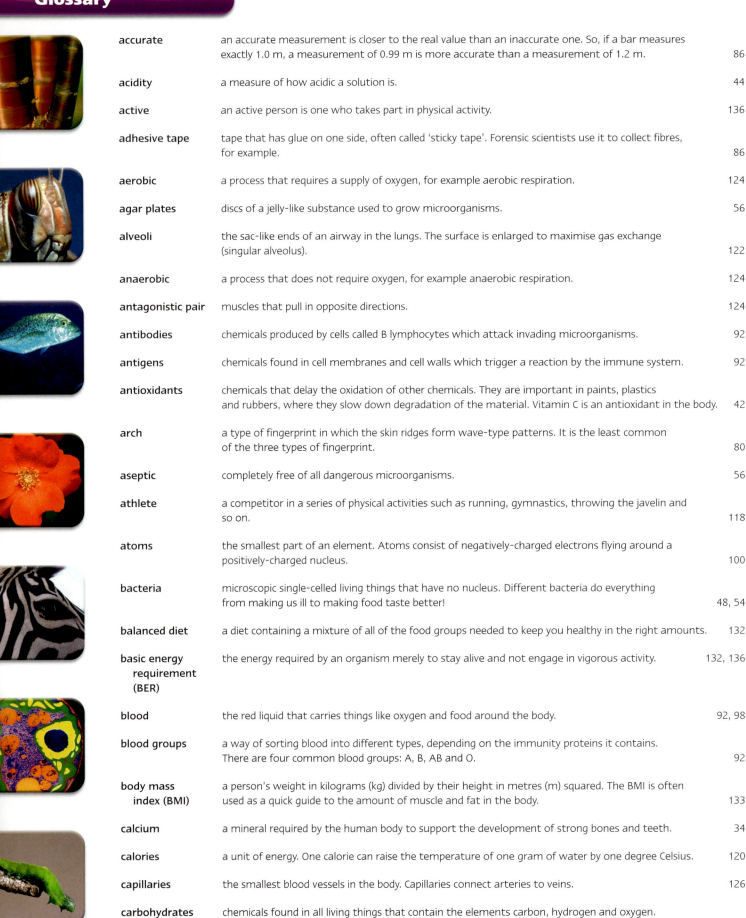

accurate	an accurate measurement is closer to the real value than an inaccurate one. So, if a bar measures exactly 1.0 m, a measurement of 0.99 m is more accurate than a measurement of 1.2 m.	86
acidity	a measure of how acidic a solution is.	44
active	an active person is one who takes part in physical activity.	136
adhesive tape	tape that has glue on one side, often called 'sticky tape'. Forensic scientists use it to collect fibres, for example.	86
aerobic	a process that requires a supply of oxygen, for example aerobic respiration.	124
agar plates	discs of a jelly-like substance used to grow microorganisms.	56
alveoli	the sac-like ends of an airway in the lungs. The surface is enlarged to maximise gas exchange (singular alveolus).	122
anaerobic	a process that does not require oxygen, for example anaerobic respiration.	124
antagonistic pair	muscles that pull in opposite directions.	124
antibodies	chemicals produced by cells called B lymphocytes which attack invading microorganisms.	92
antigens	chemicals found in cell membranes and cell walls which trigger a reaction by the immune system.	92
antioxidants	chemicals that delay the oxidation of other chemicals. They are important in paints, plastics and rubbers, where they slow down degradation of the material. Vitamin C is an antioxidant in the body.	42
arch	a type of fingerprint in which the skin ridges form wave-type patterns. It is the least common of the three types of fingerprint.	80
aseptic	completely free of all dangerous microorganisms.	56
athlete	a competitor in a series of physical activities such as running, gymnastics, throwing the javelin and so on.	118
atoms	the smallest part of an element. Atoms consist of negatively-charged electrons flying around a positively-charged nucleus.	100
bacteria	microscopic single-celled living things that have no nucleus. Different bacteria do everything from making us ill to making food taste better!	48, 54
balanced diet	a diet containing a mixture of all of the food groups needed to keep you healthy in the right amounts.	132
basic energy requirement (BER)	the energy required by an organism merely to stay alive and not engage in vigorous activity.	132, 136
blood	the red liquid that carries things like oxygen and food around the body.	92, 98
blood groups	a way of sorting blood into different types, depending on the immunity proteins it contains. There are four common blood groups: A, B, AB and O.	92
body mass index (BMI)	a person's weight in kilograms (kg) divided by their height in metres (m) squared. The BMI is often used as a quick guide to the amount of muscle and fat in the body.	133
calcium	a mineral required by the human body to support the development of strong bones and teeth.	34
calories	a unit of energy. One calorie can raise the temperature of one gram of water by one degree Celsius.	120
capillaries	the smallest blood vessels in the body. Capillaries connect arteries to veins.	126
carbohydrates	chemicals found in all living things that contain the elements carbon, hydrogen and oxygen. Sugars are carbohydrates that dissolve in water and taste sweet. Starches are carbohydrates that cannot dissolve in water and do not taste sweet.	30, 136

carbon dioxide	a gas containing only carbon and oxygen. Its chemical formula is CO_2.	102
cardiovascular system	the lungs, heart and blood vessels.	122

cast	a technique using a mould to hold a liquid while it sets to form a solid. The solid will have the same shape as the original mould. Forensic scientist make casts of footprints at a crime scene by using the footprint as a mould.	90
cells	the smallest parts of a living thing. Cells usually have a nucleus and cytoplasm and a range of other parts. Cells of some types of microorganisms do not have a proper nucleus.	93
charged	a body is charged if it holds an electrical charge – this can be positive or negative.	100
colourings	chemicals added to foods or other substances to give them a particular colour.	42
comparison microscope	a special kind of microscope that can compare two fields of view easily. Often used to check one specimen against a standard image.	90

composite	a substance made of two or more different substances mixed together.	142–145
compounds	compounds are groups of atoms bound together, in fixed proportions, by chemical bonds. Compounds have different chemical and physical properties from the elements they contain.	102
compressive strength	the ability to resist compressive forces.	142
contaminate	to add something, usually toxic, to another substance. For example, milk can sometimes be contaminated by small amounts of antibiotics used to treat cows.	78

contamination	the presence of an unwanted, often toxic, chemical in another substance.	56
contract	to get smaller.	124
covalent bond	a covalent bond is a link between two atoms where electrons move around both atoms in the pair. Covalent bonds tend to be strong bonds and form between non-metals.	102
crime scene	the area where a crime has been committed.	76–79, 86

deficiency disease	an illness in plants and animals caused by the lack of a specific nutrient.	32
density	the mass of an object divided by its volume. Solids tend to be denser than liquids and much denser than gases.	142–147
deoxyribonucleic acid (DNA)	the molecule that carries genetic information in animals and higher plants.	74, 98
diet diary	a record of all of the food and drink consumed by someone over a period of time.	134

dietary recall	one of the ways in which an athlete monitors what they eat. It involves remembering and recording everything they have eaten in the past 24 hours.	134
dietician	a medically trained person with a special interest and expertise in people's diets.	34, 120
DNA profiling	cataloguing the DNA present in an individual.	98
E number	a code number for approved food additives. For example, the E number for vitamin C is E300.	42
electrolytes	liquids that carry an electric current.	134
electrons	a small, negatively-charged particle that orbits around the nucleus of an atom.	102

electrophoresis	a process in which molecules of different charges are separated by applying a high voltage across a strip of material, on which a mixture containing the molecules is placed.	98

Glossary

identify	to find the correct name for something. Ecologists often have to identify the plants or animals living in an area.	100
impartial	unbiased.	74
insoluble	a substance that will not dissolve. Something that is insoluble in water may be soluble in other liquids.	104

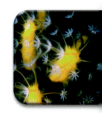

insulation	material that slows down the movement of energy, typically used with respect to heat and electricity.	146
insulin	a hormone secreted by cells in the pancreas. Insulin encourages cells to take up glucose and so reduces blood sugar levels.	126
intensive	to maximise the productivity of a piece of land or an animal.	58
ions	charged particles made when an atom, or group of atoms, gains or loses electrons.	100
isotonic sports drinks	drinks with the same water potential as the blood.	135

kilocalorie	1000 calories.	133
kilojoule	1000 joules.	133
lactic acid	a toxic chemical produced by anaerobic respiration in animals.	125
loop	a type of fingerprint in which the skin ridges form loop-type patterns.	80
lung capacity	the amount of air you can hold in your lungs.	122
lungs	the lungs swap carbon dioxide in the blood for oxygen in the air.	119

marketing	informing potential customers about a particular product or service.	37
materials scientists	scientists who specialise in the development and use of new materials.	121
microbiologists	scientists who study microorganisms.	48
microorganisms	very small living things, only visible under a microscope. Most are harmless, some are useful and some cause serious illnesses.	49, 55

microscope	a device you can use to see very small things.	87
minerals	mineral nutrients in our diet are things like calcium and iron. They are simple chemicals needed for health.	30
muscles	organs that can contract; they are joined to bones at each end by tendons.	119, 125
natural fertilisers	fertilisers like manure that have not been made by human beings.	59

nutrients	another word for food groups like carbohydrates and fats. Plants need certain chemicals from the soil, and these are called mineral nutrients.	31, 45, 59, 119
nutrition	the way a living organism gets food to keep itself alive and healthy.	121
nutritional information	information about the nutrients present in food.	135

organic	organic food and farming is a system that avoids the use of modern, synthetic chemicals.	58
oxygen debt	the amount of oxygen needed to clear the lactic acid produced by anaerobic respiration during vigorous exercise in animals.	125

Glossary

pancreas	organ in the abdomen that produces enzymes to break down food. It also contains the islets of Langerhans, small groups of cells that produce the hormone insulin.	127
phosphorus	a non-metal that bursts into flame when exposed to the air.	35
plasma	the liquid portion of the blood.	93
platelets	small, subcellular bodies in the blood concerned with clotting.	93
polarising microscope	a microscope that uses polarised light to make structures in the cell look clearer.	90
polymer	single large molecules formed by joining together monomers.	143, 147
polypropylene	a polymer made of propylene. It is a common plastic.	147
preservatives	chemicals added to foods or other substances to prevent them decaying.	43
proteins	a food group found in meat, cheese and beans. Protein is important for your body's growth.	31, 45
Public Health Inspectors	officials employed by the government who check on the safety of premises like restaurants, factories and theme parks.	55
Recommended Dietary Allowance (RDA)	the RDA of a foodstuff, perhaps a vitamin, is the amount dieticians recommend for a healthy diet.	135
recovery rate	the time taken for breathing to return to its resting rate after exercise.	125
reducing sugar	a sugar that turns orange-brown with Benedict's solution.	45
Reference Nutritional Intake (RNI)	the recommended daily intake for a variety of nutrients, sometimes called the Recommended Dietary Allowance or RDA.	46
refractive index	a measure of how much a sample of glass or other transparent medium will bend light.	89
respiration	the chemical process that makes energy from food in the cells in your body. All living things must respire.	31, 123–127
rickets	a disease caused by a lack of essential nutrients, which leads to bent bones in the legs.	32
Scene of Crime Officers (SOCOs)	police officers with scientific training who collect forensic evidence at a crime scene.	75, 79
scurvy	a disease caused by lack of vitamin C. Scurvy makes your gums red, your teeth fall out and your skin unhealthy.	33
sell-by date	a date after which it is illegal to sell perishable foods because they might have degraded.	45
serial dilution	a series of dilutions to produce a range of solutions with different concentrations.	57
sharing	a covalent bond is formed when two atoms share electrons, that is, they both use them.	103
shelf life	the time a product, usually a food product, can be safely stored and offered for sale on a shop shelf.	43
simple molecules	molecules with a few atoms, for example carbon dioxide or methane.	103
solutions	a solution forms when something dissolves in something else. For example, sugar dissolving in water creates a sugar solution.	105
spirometer	an instrument for measuring the volume of air entering and leaving the lungs.	123
sports scientist	a scientist with particular interest and skill in the effects of activity on the human body.	119–121

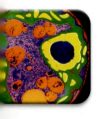

starch	large carbohydrate molecules made up of small sugar molecules joined together in a chain. Many plants use starches as an energy store in fruits and seeds.	45
streak plate	an agar plate that has had microorganisms spread across it with an inoculating loop or other device.	57
striation marks	stripes of colour, perhaps in a rock or in the tissues of a muscle.	91
sub-atomic	smaller than an atom.	101
suspect	a person who police think might have committed a crime.	77, 91

suspended matter	small particles too large to dissolve but too small to settle out of a liquid. Liquids with suspended matter often look cloudy.	47
sweat	liquid produced by the skin, which cools you down when it evaporates.	127
sweeteners	chemicals added to foods to make them taste sweeter.	43
synthetic	made by human beings. For example, plastics are synthetic compounds that do not occur naturally in nature.	145

temperature	a measure of how hot something is.	127, 147
tensile strength	a measure of how strong an object is when pulled in two directions.	143–145
thermal insulator	a substance that resists the flow of heat.	147
thickeners	chemicals added to foodstuffs to make them less liquid.	43
thorax	the chest region.	123

tidal volume	the volume of air a person breathes in and out when they are resting.	123
titration	mixing of liquids in carefully measured amounts to find the amount of one substance needed to react with a measured amount of another.	47
toxins	harmful substances produced by a microbe.	55
trace	a very small amount of something. For example, a trace of blood left at a crime scene.	77, 93
training	the regime athletes follow to teach their bodies to perform better in a range of activities.	119–121

tyre	a rubber, usually air-filled, object that is placed around a metal frame to improve road-holding and ride comfort in vehicles.	91
unbiased	not giving an unfair advantage to any group in a test.	75
Universal Indicator paper	an indicator paper that changes colour in solutions of different pH.	105
urine	liquid made by your kidneys to get rid of waste from the blood.	127
victims	people who have been hurt by a crime.	77

vitamins	chemicals needed by the body in very small amounts to keep it healthy.	31–34
water	a clear liquid found in all living things. Water contains the elements hydrogen and oxygen and has the chemical formula H_2O.	103, 127
whorl	a curl or spiral pattern in fingerprints.	81
yeast	a unicellular fungus used extensively in the brewing and baking industries.	49

Acknowledgements

The authors and publishers are grateful to the following for permission to reproduce photographs. Whilst every effort has been made to trace the copyright holders, in cases where this has been unsuccessful or if any have been inadvertently overlooked, the Publishers will be pleased to make the necessary arrangements at the first opportunity.

contents ©Dr Kari Lounatmaa/SPL, ©Ian Bracegirdle/istockphotos.com, ©Dan Brandenburg/istockphotos.com; p.6 tl ©BSIP Chassenet/SPL, tr ©Ed Hidden/istockphotos.com, bl ©Laguna Design/SPL, br ©Kristen Johansen/istockphotos.com; p.7 tl ©TEK Image/SPL, tr ©David Scharf/SPL, bl ©Peter Adams/istockphotos.com, br ©Bill Barksdale/AGStock/SPL; p.8/9 background ©Alfred Pasieka/SPL; p.8 tl ©Perttu Sironen/istockphotos.com, tr ©Mark Evans/istockphotos.com, bl ©Eva Serrabassa/istockphotos.com, br ©Yvonne, Chamberlain/istockphotos.com; p.9 tl ©Professors P M Motta & S Correr/SPL, tr ©Adam Waliczek/istockphotos.com, bl ©Pedro Diaz/istockphotos.com, br ©Stijn Peeters/istockphotos.com; p.10/11 background ©Ian McDonnell/istockphotos.com; p.10 tl ©istockphotos.com, tr ©Sawomir Fajer/istockphotos.com, bl Kelly Cline/istockphotos.com, br ©Matthew Cole/istockphotos.com; p.11 tl ©Gregg Cerenzio/istockphotos.com, tr ©Karina Tischlinger/istockphotos.com, bl ©Thomas Brostrom/istockphotos.com, br ©Joe Gough/istockphotos.com; p.14 br ©Joseph Abbott/istockphotos.com; p.15 bl ©Nicholas Sutcliffe/istockphotos.com, r ©Lisa Barber/Alamy; p.16 tr ©Jason Hoffman/istockphotos.com, bl ©istockphotos.com; p.17 ©Kelvin Wakefield/istockphotos.com; p.20 ©John Greim/SPL; p.22 l ©Antonia Reeve/SPL, r ©Dr P. Marazzi/SPL; p.23 ©Steve Horrell/SPL; p.24 t ©Per Lindgren/Rex Features, b ©Mann McGowan Fabrications Ltd, used with kind permission; p.25 tr ©Mark Hayes/istockphotos.com; p.27 tr ©Jupiterimagescorporation/Photos.com, br ©Ralph Martens/istockphotos.com; p.28/29 background ©Maximilian Stock Ltd/SPL; p.30 1 ©Patrik Giardino/Corbis; p.31 2 ©Sheila Terry/SPL; p.32 1 ©Michael Reusse/Westend61/Alamy, 2 ©Sheila Terry/SPL; p.33 3 ©Dr Mark J. Winter/SPL; 4 l ©Biophoto Associates/SPL, r ©Jim Stevenson/SPL, 5 ©Biophoto Associates/SPL; p.34 1 ©Paul Bricknell/Dorling Kindersley/Getty Images; p.35 2 ©Scott Camazine, Sue Trainor/SPL; p.37 2 l ©Roy Morsch/Corbis, r ©Cruz Puga/istockphotos.com, 3 ©Voisin/Phanie/Rex Features; p.38/39 ©Jupiterimages2007photos.com; p.38 inset ©Penny Fowler; p.42 1 ©Andrew McClenaghan/SPL; p.43 2 ©BSIP, MENDIL/SPL, 3 ©Maximilian Stock Ltd/SPL, 4 ©Foodfolio/Alamy; p.44 1 ©Tony Craddock/SPL; p.47 3 ©Andrew Lambert Photography/SPL; p.49 5 ©Sotiris Zafeiris/SPL, 6 ©Dr Kari Lounatmaa/SPL; p.54 1 ©Science Pictures Ltd/SPL, table 1 t ©Dr Gary Gaugler/SPL, c ©Dr Gary Gaugler/SPL, b ©Dr Linda Stannard, UCT/SPL; p.55 2 ©Adrienne Hart-Davis/SPL; p.56 1 ©TEK Image/SPL, 2 ©BSIP, Beranger/SPL; p.57 ©John Durham/SPL; p.59 1 ©Harris Barnes Jr/AgStock/SPL, 2 l ©Marcelo Brodsky/SPL, r ©Macduff Everton/Corbis, 3 ©Geoff Tompkinson/SPL, 4 ©Dr Jeremy Burgess/SPL; p.60 1 ©Andrew Syred/SPL; p.61 4 ©George W. Miller/SPL, 5 Ed Young/AgStock/SPL; p.62/63 ©Fred Goldstein/istockphotos.com; p.68 l ©Marco Regalia/istockphotos.com, cb ©Stephan Hoerold/istockphotos.com; p.69 ©Volker Steger, Peter Arnold Inc./SPL; p.72/73 ©Michael Donne, University of Manchester/SPL; p.74 1 ©Sion Touhig/Corbis; p.75 2 ©Charity Myers/istockphotos.com, 3 ©Bettmann/Corbis; p.76 1 ©Jupiter Images/Photos.com; p.77 5 ©Reuters/Corbis; p.78 1 ©George Clerk/istockphotos.com, 2 ©Jupiter Images/Photos.com, 3 ©George Cairns/istockphotos.com; p.79 4 ©TEK Image/SPL; p.80 1 ©Ian Bracegirdle/istockphotos.com; p.81 3 ©Brandon Alms/istockphotos.com; p.86 1 r ©Alvaro Pantoja/istockphotos.com; p.88 1 ©Sean Nel/istockphotos.com; p.89 6 ©David Parker/SPL; p.90 1 ©David McCarthy/SPL; p.91 2 ©Scott Elliott/istockphotos.com; p.92 1 ©How Stuff Works, used with kind permission; p.98 1 ©Dan Brandenburg/istockphotos.com, 2 ©Andrei Tchernov/istockphotos.com, 3 ©Carl Goodman/SPL; p.99 4 ©John McLean/SPL; p.100 1 ©Maurice van der Velden/istockphotos.com; p.101 4 ©Laguna Design/SPL; p.102 1 ©Andrzej Tokarski/istockphotos.com; p.103 5 ©Michael Donne/SPL; p.104 1 ©Dragan Trifunovic/istockphotos.com; p.112 t ©George Cairns/istockphotos.com, c ©Andrei Tchernov/istockphotos.com; p.116/117 ©Mike Blake/Reuters/Corbis; p.118 1 ©Ana Abejon/istockphotos.com, 2 ©Peter Chen/istockphotos.com, 3 ©millsrymer/CSP/istockphotos.com; p.119 ©Bettmann/Corbis; p.120 1 ©Pavel Losevsky/istockphotos.com, 2 ©Eliza Snow/istockphotos.com; p.121 3 ©Underwood & Underwood/Corbis, 4 ©Cheryl Quigley; p.122 1 ©Jaimie D. Travis/istockphotos.com; p.124 1 ©Galina Barskaya/istockphotos.com, 2 ©Kateryna Govorushchenko/istockphotos.com; p.125 4 & 5 ©Jupiterimages/photos.com; p.126 1 ©Shannon Rush/istockphotos.com, 3 ©Jon Rasmussen/istockphotos.com; p.128/129 ©Robert Brown/istockphotos.com; p.132 1 ©Kelly Cline/istockphotos.com, 2 ©Elena Aliaga/istockphotos.com; p.133 3 ©Michael Donne/SPL; p.134 1 ©Edward Lettau/SPL, 2 © James Boulett/istockphotos.com; p.135 3 ©Leland Beaumont/istockphotos.com, 4 ©James Steidl/istockphotos.com; p.136 1 ©David Vaughan/SPL, 2 ©Jennifer Trenchard/istockphotos.com; p.137 4 ©Sue Colvil/istockphotos.com, 5 ©SBIP, Laurent/B. Hop Ame/SPL; p.138/139 ©Jupiterimages2007/photos.com; p.142 1 ©Stefan Steinbach/istockphotos.com; p.144 1 ©Galina Barskaya/istockphotos.com; p.145 2 ©Head UK Ltd, reproduced with kind permission of Head UK Ltd, 3 ©Cordelia Molloy/SPL; p.146 1 ©David Brodie; p.147 2 ©N Nicholas, used with kind permission, 3 ©Bettmann/Corbis; p.148 1 ©Shaun Lowe/istockphotos.com; p.149 2 ©Royalty Free/Corbis, Jerome Prevost/Source/Corbis; p.150/151 ©Martin Kawalski/istockphotos.com; p.156 r ©Ronald Manera/istockphotos.com, bc ©Justin Allfree/istockphotos.com; p.157 ©Dennys Bisogno/istockphotos.com; p.165 ©George Ranalli/SPL; p. 163, 167 ©Dr Jeremy Burgess/SPL; p.163/167 ©Dr Kari Lounatmaa/SPL; p.162, 166 ©Dr Jeremy Burgess/SPL